Hybrid Cloud for Architects

Build robust hybrid cloud solutions using AWS and OpenStack

Alok Shrivastwa

BIRMINGHAM - MUMBAI

Hybrid Cloud for Architects

Reviewers: David Duncan, Ganesh Raja
Commissioning Editor: Gebin George
Acquisition Editor: Rohit Rajkumar
Content Development Editor: Nithin Varghese
Technical Editor: Mohit Hassija
Copy Editors: Safis Editing, Laxmi Subramanian
Project Coordinator: Virginia Dias
Proofreader: Safis Editing
Indexer: Rekha Nair
Graphics: Tom Scaria
Production Coordinator: Nilesh Mohite

First published: February 2018

Production reference: 1220218

Published by Packt Publishing Ltd.
Livery Place
35 Livery Street
Birmingham
B3 2PB, UK.

ISBN 978-1-78862-351-3

www.packtpub.com

`mapt.io`

Mapt is an online digital library that gives you full access to over 5,000 books and videos, as well as industry leading tools to help you plan your personal development and advance your career. For more information, please visit our website.

Why subscribe?

- Spend less time learning and more time coding with practical eBooks and Videos from over 4,000 industry professionals

- Improve your learning with Skill Plans built especially for you

- Get a free eBook or video every month

- Mapt is fully searchable

- Copy and paste, print, and bookmark content

PacktPub.com

Did you know that Packt offers eBook versions of every book published, with PDF and ePub files available? You can upgrade to the eBook version at `www.PacktPub.com` and as a print book customer, you are entitled to a discount on the eBook copy. Get in touch with us at `service@packtpub.com` for more details.

At `www.PacktPub.com`, you can also read a collection of free technical articles, sign up for a range of free newsletters, and receive exclusive discounts and offers on Packt books and eBooks.

Contributors

About the author

Alok Shrivastwa is a technologist from India, currently working as the director of special projects for Microland in the CMD's office. He currently runs special projects on cloud technologies. Having worked at multiple enterprises of varied sizes, designing and implementing solutions, public and private clouds, and integrations, he has created a myriad number of tools and intellectual properties in the operationalization of emerging technologies. He has authored two books on OpenStack alongside several white papers and blogs on technology, in addition to writing poems in Hindi.

> *We as humans need contrast, without which we cannot perceive. Because of this, to show something in a good light, something has to be made the villain. This book is about being pragmatic when looking at the cloud. I thank God for the perspective, and my family—my mother, father, sisters and my niece, Aarya—who helped me see it. I am thankful to each and every person who I meet and learn from.*

About the reviewer

David Duncan is a partner solutions architect at Amazon Web Services who specializes in enabling open source platform partners. He focuses on enabling Linux support on Amazon EC2, cloud native deployments, and hybrid cloud workloads with operating system partners such as Red Hat OpenShift, SUSE Cloud Application Platform, and the Canonical distribution of Kubernetes. David is a coauthor of the book *AWS Quick Start for Red Hat OpenShift*.

Packt is searching for authors like you

If you're interested in becoming an author for Packt, please visit `authors.packtpub.com` and apply today. We have worked with thousands of developers and tech professionals, just like you, to help them share their insight with the global tech community. You can make a general application, apply for a specific hot topic that we are recruiting an author for, or submit your own idea.

Table of Contents

Preface

The book takes us on a journey of architecting, building, and operating a hybrid cloud while taking a very pragmatic approach towards it. The book starts by defining the different demographics of the cloud and the different use cases that need to be solved. It then introduces two modes of building a hybrid cloud, with the CMP and the other with containers—along with the use cases that each of them addresses. The book finally drops into operational mode with topics such as DevOps, monitoring, and security considerations in the hybrid cloud.

Who this book is for

This book is targeted at cloud architects, cloud solution providers, DevOps engineers, or any working stakeholder who wants to learn about the hybrid cloud architecture. A basic understanding of public and private clouds is desirable.

What this book covers

Chapter 1, *Introducing Hybrid Cloud*, deals with the definitions and demographics of the cloud, the differences between service down and infrastructure up cloud, and its examples.

Chapter 2, *Hybrid Cloud – Why Does It Matter?*, starts with adoption statistics of the hybrid cloud and moves on to drivers for cloud adoption, public cloud benefits, and its shortcomings. Finally, we introduce a case for hybrid cloud and how to maximize the benefits using the best of both worlds.

Chapter 3, *Hybrid Cloud Building Blocks*, introduces the building blocks of the hybrid cloud using an example of a web application, use cases that potentially will need a hybrid cloud, making applications suitable for a hybrid cloud using decoupling, and services that are used to enable the hybrid cloud.

Chapter 4, *Architecting the Underpinning Services*, covers the concepts of networking, DNS systems, IAM systems, application components, and choosing the appropriate components for the use with a hybrid cloud.

Chapter 5, *Hybrid Cloud Deployment – Architecture and Preparation*, covers the concepts of AWS, architecting an AWS environment, the basic design of an OpenStack environment, setting up a DevStack, and connectivity between the cloud environments.

Chapter 6, *Building a Traditional CMP-Based Hybrid Cloud*, starts with AWS's storage gateway and use cases in the hybrid cloud scenario, the concepts of CMP, setting up Docker, and running a ManageIQ container in Docker.

Chapter 7, *Building a Containerized Hybrid Cloud*, introduces the basics of container orchestration platforms, an introduction to Kubernetes, deploying Kubernetes using Juju, and closes with using the kubefed project to federate a hybrid cloud based on Kubernetes.

Chapter 8, *Using Prebuilt Hybrid Cloud Solution*, introduces products that are available from different providers, including AzureStack and Project Omni.

Chapter 9, *DevOps in the Hybrid Cloud*, deals with the traditional development cycle and the steps involved, along with the concepts of DevOps and NoOps. We look at the introduction to IaaC, templatizer, and configuration management systems and their roles in the development cycle. We take an example of Terraform and its deployment with a sample to solidify the concepts of IaaC. Also, deploy Ansible and a sample to solidify the concepts of configuration management.

Chapter 10, *Monitoring the Hybrid Cloud*, introduces the basics of monitoring, along with Prometheus and Grafana, to help us monitor the hybrid cloud.

Chapter 11, *Security in a Hybrid Cloud*, starts with the concepts of security and compliance standards, and moves on to taking HIPAA as an example to elucidate some of the best practices that need to be used.

To get the most out of this book

While a simple reading of the book will impart the different architectural and cloud concepts to the reader, in order to follow along, ensure that you have the following:

- An internet connection to download the software.
- A Ubuntu 16.04 machine to act as the management system.
- A fully functioning OpenStack deployment or a Ubuntu 16.04 machine to run DevStack.

- AWS user account—if you don't have the user account, ensure that you have your credit card ready in order to open a free account. (Remember that while we have taken care to use the *free-tier* systems in AWS, make sure you use the appropriate instance sizes and AMI IDs if you are creating the environment in a different region).

Download the example code files

You can download the example code files for this book from your account at `www.packtpub.com`. If you purchased this book elsewhere, you can visit `www.packtpub.com/support` and register to have the files emailed directly to you.

You can download the code files by following these steps:

1. Log in or register at `www.packtpub.com`.
2. Select the **SUPPORT** tab.
3. Click on **Code Downloads & Errata**.
4. Enter the name of the book in the **Search** box and follow the onscreen instructions.

Once the file is downloaded, please make sure that you unzip or extract the folder using the latest version of:

- WinRAR/7-Zip for Windows
- Zipeg/iZip/UnRarX for Mac
- 7-Zip/PeaZip for Linux

The code bundle for the book is also hosted on GitHub at `https://github.com/PacktPublishing/Hybrid-Cloud-for-Architects`. In case there's an update to the code, it will be updated on the existing GitHub repository.

We also have other code bundles from our rich catalog of books and videos available at `https://github.com/PacktPublishing/`. Check them out!

Download the color images

We also provide a PDF file that has color images of the screenshots/diagrams used in this book. You can download it here: `https://www.packtpub.com/sites/default/files/downloads/HybridCloudforArchitects_ColorImages.pdf`.

Conventions used

There are a number of text conventions used throughout this book.

CodeInText: Indicates code words in text, database table names, folder names, filenames, file extensions, pathnames, dummy URLs, user input, and Twitter handles. Here is an example: "Default values are port 80 for HTTP, port 443 for HTTPS."

A block of code is set as follows:

```
provider "aws" {
 access_key = "<Enter Access Key Here>"
 secret_key = "<Enter Secret Key Here>"
 region = "us-east-1"
}
```

When we wish to draw your attention to a particular part of a code block, the relevant lines or items are set in bold:

```
provider "aws" {
 access_key = "<Enter Access Key Here>"
 secret_key = "<Enter Secret Key Here>"
 region = "us-east-1"
}
```

Any command-line input or output is written as follows:

```
sudo cp terraform /usr/local/bin
```

Bold: Indicates a new term, an important word, or words that you see onscreen. For example, words in menus or dialog boxes appear in the text like this. Here is an example: "Gartner introduced the Bimodal IT concept and coined two terms called **mode-1** and **mode-2** of the development."

 Warnings or important notes appear like this.

 Tips and tricks appear like this.

Get in touch

Feedback from our readers is always welcome.

General feedback: Email `feedback@packtpub.com` and mention the book title in the subject of your message. If you have questions about any aspect of this book, please email us at `questions@packtpub.com`.

Errata: Although we have taken every care to ensure the accuracy of our content, mistakes do happen. If you have found a mistake in this book, we would be grateful if you would report this to us. Please visit `www.packtpub.com/submit-errata`, selecting your book, clicking on the Errata Submission Form link, and entering the details.

Piracy: If you come across any illegal copies of our works in any form on the Internet, we would be grateful if you would provide us with the location address or website name. Please contact us at `copyright@packtpub.com` with a link to the material.

If you are interested in becoming an author: If there is a topic that you have expertise in and you are interested in either writing or contributing to a book, please visit `authors.packtpub.com`.

Reviews

Please leave a review. Once you have read and used this book, why not leave a review on the site that you purchased it from? Potential readers can then see and use your unbiased opinion to make purchase decisions, we at Packt can understand what you think about our products, and our authors can see your feedback on their book. Thank you!

For more information about Packt, please visit `packtpub.com`.

1
Introducing Hybrid Cloud

The word *cloud* has been commonplace in the industry and marketplace for over a decade. In its modern usage, it was first used in August of 2006, when Eric Schmidt of Google used it to describe an emergent new model (Source: Technology Review). However, now thanks to a, then, little-known company called **Amazon Web Services** (**AWS**), it has become immensely famous.

Did you know?

Amazon started work on its cloud in the year 2000; the key years in its development were 2003, 2004, and 2006. In 2004, the AWS, or web services at the time, were simply a group of disparate APIs and not a full-blown IaaS/PaaS service as it is today.

The first service to be launched in 2003 was a **Simple Queue Service** (**SQS**) and then later, S3 and EC2 were added. In 2006, the cloud as we know it today gained popularity.

Once the term *cloud computing* became a part of common IT parlance, there was no dearth of definitions. Almost everyone had something to sell, and added their own spin on the terminology.

In this chapter, we will attempt to decipher this different terminology in relation to the definitions of the different clouds.

If you are wondering why this is important, it is to make and maintain the clarity of context in future chapters, as new concepts emerge and are commingled in the grand scheme of architecting the hybrid cloud.

Did you know?
The term cloud computing was first used in 1996, by a group of executives at Compaq to describe the future of the internet business.

- Technology Review

In the remaining part of the chapter, we take a look at different definitions of the cloud and the different products used.

The cloud's demographics

In trying to navigate through the maze of the several definition's that are available, it is clear that there are various ways in which we can take a look at clouds, however, we will focus on the main ones and simplify them for our understanding.

As a first step, let us define what could pass as cloud computing. The Wikipedia definition is as follows:

> *"Cloud computing is an (IT) paradigm, a model for enabling ubiquitous access to shared pools of configurable resources (such as computer networks, servers, storage, applications and services), which can be rapidly provisioned with minimal management effort, often over the Internet"*

If we look at that statement from a technical standpoint, it would be fair to say that in order for something to be referred to as cloud computing, it must at least possess the following characteristics:

- Self-service (reduces wait time to get resources provisioned)
- Shared, standard, consistent (shared pools of configurable resources)
- Cross-domain automation (rapid provisioning)
- Consumption based chargeback and billing

The three main ways in which we can take a look at dissecting the clouds are as follows:

- Based on abstraction
- Based on the services offered
- Based on the consumers of the services

Based on abstraction

The underlying principle of cloud is **abstraction**; how it is abstracted determines a lot of its feature sets and behavior. However, this aspect of the cloud is little-known and often ignored. It *only* becomes evident when dealing with different kinds of clouds from different providers.

We shall delve into the details and nuances. For starters, these are:

- Service down clouds
- Infrastructure up clouds

To understand these better, let's take a look at the following stack, (which is used to run an application). The stack assumes a virtualized infrastructure being used to run the application.

In the event of an application running on bare-metal, the **Virtual Machine** and the **Hypervisor** layers will be absent, but the remainder of the stack will still be in play.

In traditional IT businesses, different teams manage different aspects of this stack. For example, the **Infrastructure** management team manages the underlying hardware and its configuration, the **Virtualization** team manages the **Virtual Machine** and the **Hypervisor**, the **Platform** team manages the **Middleware**, the **Operating System** teams manage the **Operating System** and finally the **Application** team will manage the **Application** and the data on top of the stack.

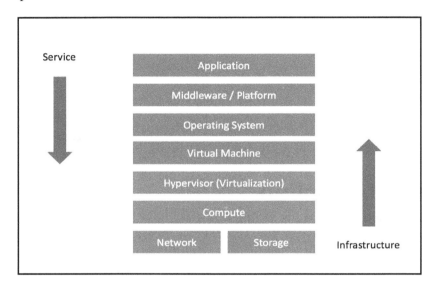

Now, from the perspective of the **Infrastructure** management team, they see that the application runs on the **Virtual Machine** and from the perspective of the **Application** developers, they simply see that the **Infrastructure** team is providing a combination of three services namely **Network**, **Compute**, and **Storage**. This is the essence of the split.

Service down clouds

The **service down** approach of building clouds was pioneered by AWS. This approach was created *for developers, by developers*. The salient feature of this kind of cloud is the fact that everything is a Lego block, which can be combined in different ways in order to achieve a desired function.

In the service down approach, the **Create, Read, Update, and Delete** (**CRUD**) operations on these Lego blocks are normally done using API calls, so that developers can easily request the resources they need using programming and not by operations.

In the service down cloud, everything, such as compute (RAM and CPU), storage, network, and so on is a separate service and can be combined to give us a **Virtual Machine**. The following diagram shows the three blocks (the service names used are AWS services, however all service down clouds will have equivalents) coming together in order to create a traditional equivalent of a virtual machine:

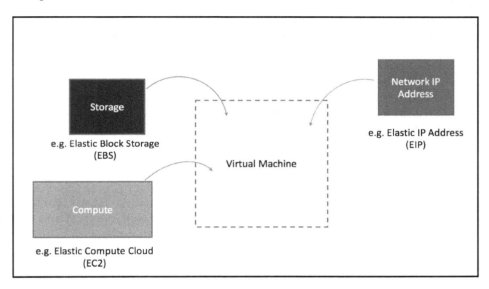

The Lego block idea works on a second level, which means you are free to move this between the different virtual machines. In the following diagram, as an example, you can see that the **Storage** 1 of **Virtual Machine 1** is being remapped to **Virtual Machine 2**, using API calls, which is unheard of when we take into account the traditional infrastructure:

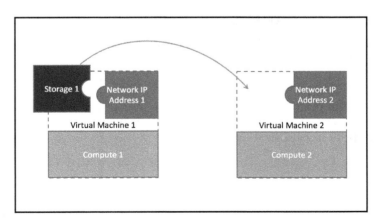

The examples of this kind of abstraction are seen in Hyperscale Clouds such as AWS, Azure, and Google Cloud Platform. However, OpenStack is also designed as a service down cloud.

Having understood the service down cloud, it is clear that this concept of Lego blocks that has enabled us to treat our infrastructure as cattle, or pets, means if one of your servers is sick you can rip it out and replace it rather than spend time troubleshooting it. You may even choose to have the same IP address and the same disk.

> **Pets versus cattle**:
> This analogy came up some time between 2011 and 2012, and describes the differences in treating your infrastructure in the cloud-based world or a traditional world. Read more about them by googling the term *Pets vs Cattle in Cloud*: http://cloudscaling.com/blog/cloud-computing/the-history-of-pets-vs-cattle/

> In brief:
>
> - Traditionally the infrastructure got treated as pets, we used to name them, nurture them, if they fell sick, we treat and care for them (troubleshoot them) and nurse them back to health.
> - These days, the cloud infrastructure gets treated as cattle, we number them, don't get attached to them, and if they fall sick, we shoot them, take their remains, and get a new one in their place.

Infrastructure up clouds

Infrastructure up, as a concept is simply appending a *orchestrator* to the existing virtualization stack that we saw before, thereby enabling self-service and increasing agility by automation.

The cloud *purists* would not even consider these clouds, but there is no denying that they exist. This concept was created to bridge the chasm that was created due to the radical shift of the paradigm of how the applications got created in the service down cloud.

In this kind of cloud, the smallest unit would request and get a virtual machine. There are several Orchestrators that would help provide these functionalities, some of the notable ones include, VMware vRealize Suite (`https://www.vmware.com/in/products/vrealize-automation.html`), Cisco CIAC (`https://www.cisco.com/c/en/us/products/cloud-systems-management/intelligent-automation-cloud/index.html`), BMC Atrium (`http://www.bmcsoftware.in/it-solutions/atrium-orchestrator.html`), to name a few.

The way this is created is by adding a *Cloud Orchestrator* solution on top of an existing virtualization environment. This provides features such as self-service and billing/chargeback/showback.

The **Orchestrator** then performs cross domain automation in order to provision virtual machines for the user. As you can see, in this case the life cycle management of the VM is automated, but the idea behind the provisioning has not changed so much. In the event that you decide to delete the VM, more likely than not, all the associated resources also get deleted.

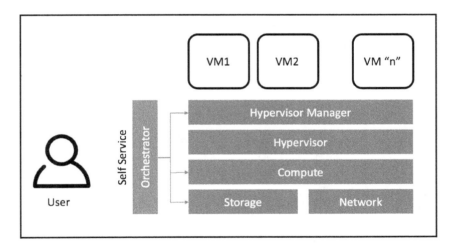

An infra-up cloud is normally characterized by the presence of a workflow Engine, which allows integration to different enterprise systems. It should be no surprise that major infra-up clouds are used in private. There are some exceptions, for example the Vodafone Secure Cloud, which is a public cloud that runs on an infra-up approach.

Differentiating service down and infrastructure up clouds

Since this might be a new concept for some of us, let's look at a comparison between service down and infra-up and the features they provide by default:

 The following table is only what is offered as default, most capabilities that are not present can be added by automation/customization in both of the fields.

Features	Infra-up	Service down
Workflow engine	Present	Not present
Infrastructure as code	Not present	Present
Self-service	Present	Present
API endpoints	Present	Present
Smallest unit that can be consumed	Virtual machine	Compute as a Service Network as a Service Storage as a Service and so on.
Chargeback/billing	Not very well-developed/monthly	Hourly, per-minute (or) per-second
Integration ability with existing enterprise tools (for example, IPAM, CMDB, and so on)	Present	Not present
PaaS services (DBaaS, Containers as a Service)	Not present	Present

Based on services offered

This is a very well-known piece of the cloud. Based on the services that a cloud offers, it could be divided into the following:

- Infrastructure as a Service (IaaS)
- Platform as a Service (PaaS)
- Software as a Service (SaaS)

While I am sure that we are familiar with these demographics of the cloud, let us take a look at the differences:

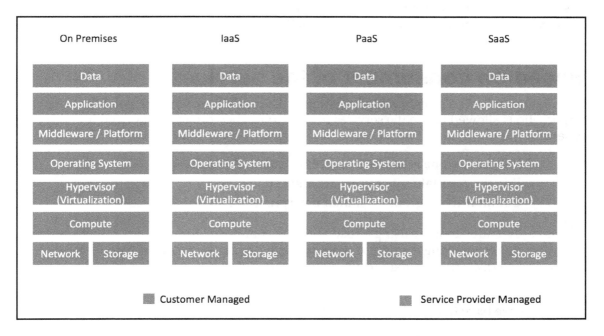

As we move from the on-premises model to IaaS, PaaS, and SaaS, the ability to customize the software decreases and standardization increases. This has led to a lot of **independent software vendors** (**ISVs**) re-writing their applications in a multi-tenanted model, and providing it to the customers in an *as a service* model.

When developing bespoke applications, organizations are choosing PaaS and IaaS instead of the traditional model, which is helping them increase agility and reduce the time to market.

Some examples of this cut of data is as follows:

Cloud Type	Examples
IaaS	OpenStack, AWS, Azure, GCP, and so on
PaaS	Cloud Foundry, AWS, Azure, GCP, and so on
SaaS	ServiceNow, Force.com, and so on

Yes, you read that right. AWS, Azure, and GCP all have IaaS and PaaS services (and arguably some SaaS services also, but more on that later).

Based on consumers of the services

This demographic is also extremely well known. Depending on who the cloud is created for, or who is allowed to use the services from a cloud, they can be categorized into three types:

- **Public**: Anyone is allowed to access
- **Private**: A certain set of users are allowed to access
- **Community**: A group of similar enterprises are allowed to access

This is easily understood by using a road analogy. A highway for example, can be used by everyone, thereby making it *public*. A road inside the grounds of a palace would be considered a *private* road. A road inside a gated community would be considered a *community* road.

Now, since we have that out of the way, let us take a look at a few examples:

- **Public cloud**: AWS, Azure, GCP, RackSpace (OpenStack), and so on
- **Private cloud**: Company X's vRealize Environment
- **Community cloud**: AWS government clouds and so on

As you will have realized, the three demographics are not mutually exclusive, which means we can use all three terms in order to describe the type of cloud.

Choosing different cloud combinations

Now we know the different combinations, let's try and answer the following questions:

- Are all the infra-up clouds private?
- Conversely, are all the service down clouds public?
- Can infrastructure up clouds be used only to serve IaaS?

You get the idea! Now, let's take a close look at the answers to these questions, and then try to decipher what circumstances might impact our decision of which cloud to use.

So a statement of fact would be, while all infra-up clouds are not private, most of them are. As an exception to this rule, a public cloud provided by Vodafone runs on VMware vRealize Suite, thereby making it an infrastructure up cloud.

The same thing is applicable to service down clouds. They are mostly used as public clouds, however, if one has a private OpenStack deployment, then it is still a service down cloud. As an example, Cisco, SAP, Intel, AT&T, and several other companies have massively scalable private clouds running on OpenStack (thereby making it a service down cloud)

While infrastructure up cloud orchestrators technically provide IaaS by default, there have been some who take it to the next level by providing **Database as a Service** (**DBaaS**) and so on.

The following section attempts to provide a few circumstances and some points you should consider when choosing the right kind of cloud:

- DevOps/NoOps:
    - In this, when we want to give more control to the development team rather than the infra team, you should choose a service down cloud
    - Depending on your current data center footprint, cost requirements, compliance requirements, scaling requirements, and so on, you would choose to use a public or a private cloud
    - Depending on the desired type of customization of the platform, one would use IaaS (more customization) or PaaS (less customization)

- Self-service:
    - Depending on complexity, you would choose infra-up (less complex) and service down (more complex)
- Integration of enterprise tools:
    - If this is our primary motive, then infra-up sounds like the most likely choice
    - The private cloud is also our only option, because public clouds are few and don't allow very much customization
- Moving to next-generation/advanced architectures:
    - If we intend to move to next generation architectures, including the likes of containerization, use of cognitive services, machine learning, artificial intelligence, and so on, we choose a service down public clouds (and Hyperscale - for example, AWS, Azure, or GCP).

We should try and escape the biases posed by the *Law of the instrument*, as stated in the following, and design clouds as per the needs and strategies of the organization, rather than what we know of them:

> *I suppose it is tempting, if the only **tool** you have is a **hammer**, to treat **everything** as if it were a **nail**.*

> *- Abraham Maslow, 1966*

We can now appreciate, the non mutual-exclusivity of the different demographics and therefore, the products in the field.

The following image shows different products in the field, and the area that they predominantly play in. We will take a look at these in detail in the next chapter, including the products and alliances in order for them to compete in the *hybrid cloud* world:

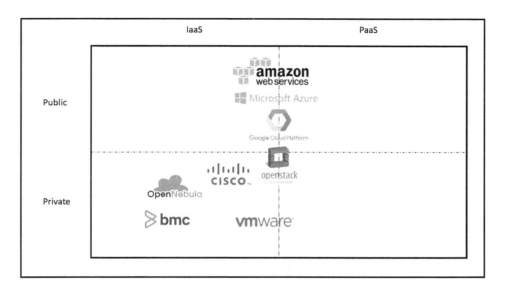

Summary

Now, to answer the question that we were asking in this chapter, the simplest definition of the hybrid cloud is that we can work with any combination of two or more of these different demographics:

The most widely accepted definition is that, the hybrid cloud is an environment comprising of a Private Cloud component (On-Premise) and a Public Cloud Component (Third party).

In this chapter, we took a look at the different ways clouds were organized, their characteristics, and the use cases.

In the remainder of this book, we will learn to architect hybrid clouds in a variety of different ways such as using a cloud management platform, using containers, and so on. For most of the book, we will be using AWS as the public cloud and OpenStack as our private cloud. We will also look at different concepts of architecting these components and samples for OpenStack and AWS.

2
Hybrid Cloud – Why Does It Matter?

Having understood the different demographics of the cloud and the definition of the hybrid cloud, naturally, the next question one might ask is, why does it matter at all? This chapter is dedicated to answering this *one question,* and looking at the perspectives and usage scenarios of the different clouds, and we will see why *hybrid cloud* is the optimal solution in most cases.

There was a time when public clouds were just taking off and were in fashion, it was like the world was split into two factions. One, we will call the *enthusiasts* and the other faction, we will call the *resistance.*

The enthusiasts were predicting the rise of the public cloud and importantly, the complete annihilation of the concept of a private data center. The resistance, on the other hand was resisting this idea, as they loved the traditional mode.

However, at the time it seemed that the enthusiasts were winning, as startups that used the public cloud were innovating at a rapid pace leaving huge enterprises in the dust. It was during this time that I came across the following quote:

> *"The cloud is like a bus, Public is not always better"*
>
> *- Unknown*

As time passed, it became clearer that in this fight of the public versus private DC/Cloud, in the long run there would be no clear winners but an emergence of a third faction, let us call them *Enlightened*, which would take the best of both worlds.

What does the world say?

Surely, the preceding statements are common sense, but what does the world say about them? In order to find out, let's take a look at a survey taken by RightScale in their *State of the Cloud* report in 2017.

The survey was conducted with over 1000 people working in several industry segments and size of companies, and the survey yielded the following (among other things):

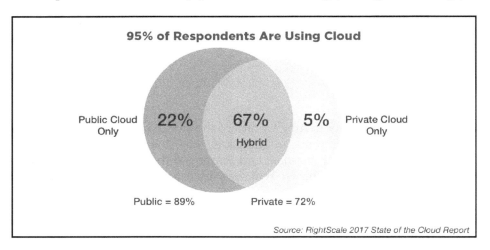

The inferences from the preceding survey are:

- Almost every one (95%) is using the cloud in some form
- Only 5% of the people are using private cloud only
- Only 22% of the people are using public cloud only
- 67% of the people are using hybrid cloud (combination of public and private)

 The **RightScale** is a cloud provider and so the report may be a little biased. However, you can read the full report from RightScale by downloading it from their website at: `https://www.rightscale.com/lp/2017-state-of-the-cloud-report`

If we compare this with the survey from last year, the number has slightly reduced owing to the reduction in people using the private cloud. However, that may be replaced by a multiple public cloud strategy (which is a different kind of strategy called multi-cloud, and beyond the purview of this book).

Pure-play public cloud strategy

The enthusiasts advocate the use of a pure-play public cloud strategy. While this has some advantages, it also comes with its share of limitations and problems, which is offset by following a hybrid cloud strategy.

Public cloud benefits

Before looking at the constraints, let's take a look at the major drivers leading to the adoption of a public cloud, which you must already be aware of:

- Need for agility in application development
- Ability to experiment without upfront costs
- Reducing operational overheads of ops teams
- Ability to consume enhanced services with little effort

Clearly, the public cloud is able to assist in all the previous points and more.

Need for agility

While at first glance, the following statement might seem odd and counter-intuitive, I would simply urge you to consider it. From time immemorial, agility has played a key role in determining a leader in a given market segment. It is just that in the traditional era, only the big enterprises could afford to have an infrastructure that gave them the agility.

However, due to various reasons, be it the fact that the entry barrier has been lowered, or the fact that the cost of capital has lowered, the advent of the public cloud has given rise to a plethora of start-ups that are challenging existing enterprises to innovate and evolve at a pace faster than ever before.

Start-ups and enterprises alike, have started using the following to reduce the time to market for the software that they are developing:

- Agile Development Methodologies (Agile versus Waterfall Model)
- DevOps - Continuous Integration and Continuous Deployment
- Infrastructure as Code (IAC)

The IAC concept was introduced by the service down cloud, which was initialized in the public cloud realm and so has a direct connection. Although the concept existed previously, DevOps became famous only in the public cloud world.

Ability to experiment without upfront cost

In order to best explain this use case, consider the scientists trying to cure deadly diseases, for which they conduct research on the human genome.

A genome, simply defined, is the blueprint of making a full organism. In humans, these genes are encoded as DNA in the 23 pairs of chromosomes.

A genome of a single individual, will take several gigabytes of storage with several million DNA. With the massive compute power that we have today, it takes up to 200 hours (8.33 days) in order to sequence a single human genome (without parallelization and excluding analysis).

Consider that a doctor needs to run a sample size of 5,000 people for lung cancer research. Without parallelization, it would take about 114 years. However, the same can now be done at a fraction of the cost in less than 7 days time using the public cloud. That's less than 30 hours per human.

The cost of genome sequencing has also dropped, from being over $100 million at the turn of the century to a little over $1,400 today.

 The report from **genome.gov** mentioning the costs of genome sequencing over the years can be found at: `https://www.genome.gov/27565109/the-cost-of-sequencing-a-human-genome/`

So, experimentation and testing with different permutations and combinations has now become a reality, without spending a fortune upfront, all thanks to hyperscale public clouds.

Reducing operational overheads

The ability to run the software on public clouds will get rid of the expenses that the company makes in several of its operations teams, including but not limited to, network, storage, operating system, virtualization, and so on.

The costs being lowered will directly impact the price (if cost plus pricing strategy is being used) and make the organization's product competitive.

Ability to consume enhanced services

Have you heard of image recognition? Yes, such as the one Facebook uses to tag you in a picture. Or would you want to build a software with inbuilt natural language processing? Yes, such as Siri, Google Assistant, Cortana, or Alexa. Do you want to use machine learning, perform sentiment analysis, and hundreds of other next-gen features without writing much code?

If so, then the only option is using the public cloud, because they practically give it away. Following is the a non-exhaustive list that shows the services offered by the three hyperscale public clouds (at the time of writing this book) in these areas:

Area	AWS	Azure	Google Cloud
Speech recognition	-Amazon Polly	-Bing Speech API	-Translation API -Speech API
Natural language processing	-Amazon Comprehend - Amazon Lex (for Chatbot)	-LUIS -Azure Bot Service -Azure Speech Recognition API	-Natural Language API
Image recognition	-Amazon Rekognition	-Emotion API -Face API -Computer Vision API	-Vision API
Machine learning	-Amazon SageMaker	-Azure Machine Learning	- Cloud DataLab - Cloud Machine Learning Services

These services are easy to consume and hence every organization, regardless of its size and expertise in these areas, can include some amount of the previously mentioned cognitive services in their applications.

Shortcomings of a public cloud

The public cloud has a few shortcomings, we call them the criticisms of the 3Cs. The 3Cs are:

- Cost
- Control/customizability
- Compliance

The preceding are common-sense, however let's look at a few case studies for each and discuss them.

Cost

If we ask you whether you would spend more living your entire life (or even a year) in a hotel or a self-owned/rented house, the answer will clearly be the latter. This is the same case in the cloud world.

The public cloud can be considered akin to a full service hotel. They will upgrade the hardware, take care of the maintenance of the servers, data center, network, and so on. They will manage the vendors and ensure the load gets taken off you.

The CoLo (Co-Location) model is comparable to a rented apartment, where you pay for the space and the basic features, but you have to bring your own furniture (hardware). This is less expensive when compared to the public cloud, but our responsibility increases multi-fold.

A private data center is similar to owning a house or an apartment. In this we are responsible for everything, and it gives us the maximum flexibility and freedom to make whatever changes we might desire. That puts an onus back on us to ensure that we know what we are doing, or hire experts temporarily (such as an architect) to help us make the changes.

As far as costs are concerned, houses are cheaper in most cases. A study on statista has shown that in the US, the average daily rate of hotels is $122.64 (https://www.statista.com/statistics/208133/us-hotel-revenue-per-available-room-by-month/) and the median square foot price in buying a home is $140 (https://www.zillow.com/home-values/), and the average house costs us over $250000.

Considering a hotel room is 100 sq-foot, the same size home (which is not easily possible) will take only 6 months to break even, and even if we use one room in the house, the hotel will break even with the home at approximately 6 years.

In order to further understand the point, let's take a look at a study done. However, remember that it is a *like to like* service comparison; we are not comparing the fancy cognitive services that can be had the public cloud.

Case in point, research by ServerPronto University and a survey conducted by 451 Research, point to the fact that a well designed (read, automated) private cloud is indeed several times cheaper (ServerPronto University claims 3X) than that of an equivalent public cloud.

Again, the internet is divided on this, however this is the truth given a certain volume. If it were not true, then AWS/Azure/GCP and the like would never make significant profits at all. In order to evade unnecessary debates, look at the following graph on the costs:

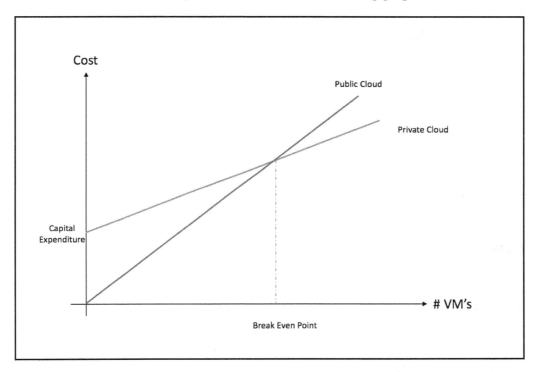

Now, let's take a look at the public cloud costs. It's a linear curve (with almost a 45 degrees slope), as we know it follows a pricing model per virtual machine (VM). As an example, if the monthly cost of a VM is $100, then 500 virtual machines a month will automatically be $50000.

 The discussion is illustrative only and the numbers quoted are examples. This also assumes that the machines are running 100% of the time.

In the private cloud, the initial capital expenditure makes it expensive initially, but for the private cloud, the additional capacity is incremental, and so the slope of the curve is a lot less than 45 degrees. For this example, we can consider it 30-35 degrees. This will ensure that there is a break-even point at which the private cloud will become cheaper than the public cloud.

Depending on what we pit the cost against (the options are number of virtual machines, % utilization of virtual machines, and virtual machines managed per engineer), the break-even point will move from the mid-hundreds to high-hundreds. The 451 Research also came to a similar conclusion.

 In the following link, Forbes talks more on the research done by 451 Research and compares running a private cloud at scale (a VM would cost $0.08 - $0.10 per hour), opposed to $0.8 (with reserved pricing)- $1.7 for the same on AWS - *that's over 10x savings even with reserved pricing*:

```
https://www.forbes.com/sites/paulmiller/2015/05/01/451-research-
unpicks-private-cloud-pricing-to-suggest-surprises/#6ad20a858d32
```

In my experience, at 400 VMs (medium- or large-sized) running at 100% utilization 24 x 7, the private cloud becomes cheaper. This number is easily achieved in any medium to large enterprise environment.

Control/customizability

The public cloud is a service offering, hence very little control can be achieved over what the company decides to use in their services (unless, you represent a significant chunk of their revenues).

The house analogy will hold good in this case as well. Consider trying to add an art piece to a hotel room. Chances are, unless you are the president of a large country, or a huge celebrity and willing to spend a fortune, the hotel room/suite will not be customizable.

The rental, might be a little more amenable to hanging an art piece. However, what about building a wall? That, your landlord may not agree with. However with your own house, you could build it anywhere you please.

One might ask, why would we need to customize? The answer is, for the most part we don't. However, if we need a certain hardware combination, then we will not be able to get that in the public cloud. While this might be bad coding practice (called **snowflake**—in short, creating unique solutions with dependencies), sometimes we can't escape it.

Compliance

The last one in our list is compliance, and this seems to get a lot of people worried, mainly due to security concerns. While public clouds are compliant to most (if not every) standard known to man, some people still get paranoid.

 The following link shows all the regulations that AWS complies with:
https://aws.amazon.com/compliance/

In order to illustrate, we will go back to our hotel analogy for the public cloud scenario. You have been assigned a room, you have no control over who gets the room next door with a shared wall. If someone plays loud music in their room, it might disturb your sleep.

So, is there a workaround? Sure there is book the whole floor.

Let me translate the preceding example into a compliance standard - HIPAA, the *Health Insurance Portability and Accountability Act* of 1996. I am not going to delve into the details of HIPAA itself as that's beyond the purview of this book, other than to say that all healthcare companies, if operating out of the United States, need to comply with it.

HIPAA has strict tenancy rules, but the cloud, by definition is multi-tenant. In order to solve this as an example, AWS has offered the **dedicated tenancy** model. In short, the hardware becomes dedicated to you (or booking the whole floor, in our analogy).

Now, while this is possible in our case, it makes the instances a little more expensive. Also a small misconfiguration might render us non-compliant in the cloud. A private cloud might be a little more resilient to this (if properly ring-fenced).

This is just one of many compliance standards that various industries use, and others like SOX (Sarbanes-Oxley), PCI DSS (Payment Card Industry - Data Security Standards), ISO (International Standards Organization), and so on have various controls for IT.

Fear of lock-in

Apart from the previously mentioned 3Cs, there is another major reason that enterprises may want to use a private cloud, or a hybrid one: to protect themselves from a lock-in.

Economically, a lock-in would take the power away from enterprises and put it in the hands of the service provider, which is not a position that the enterprise would want to take because this might mean huge economic ramifications for them in the long run.

We would like to point out that in recent years, the adoption of OpenSource has literally skyrocketed because of this fear, such as the adoption of Linux, Docker Containers, Kubernetes, and so on. It is this fear (and economically, for a good reason) that might be another driver for the enterprise to consider a hybrid cloud.

Hybrid cloud case study

In order to fully understand, let us take the case of a company called Zynga. If you are not aware of it, it's a company that makes free online games for social media platforms such as Facebook. There are several games that Zynga makes, a notable few are *Farmville, HitItRich Cityville, Poker, Mafia Wars,* and so on.

If you are on Facebook, you must have played some of them. If you haven't, then you must have at least received a lot of requests from these games through your friends. At one point, Zynga were adding five new players a second.

When it was founded over a decade ago, in April of 2007, it did not have enough capital to start a data center of its own, and the natural fit was the public cloud. In 2009, Farmville had 10 million active daily users (running over 10000 instances).

 Refer to the case study of AWS and Zynga at: `https://aws.amazon.com/solutions/case-studies/zynga/`

In 2011, Zynga built its own data centers and hosted its private cloud, zCloud, for simple cost reasons, as discussed in a previous part of this chapter.

In 2015, it returned to AWS (to innovate for the mobile platform) and eventually started using both the public and private cloud in a way so as to maximize cost benefits and innovation, therefore creating a hybrid cloud set-up.

Summary – maximizing benefits

Having understood the different drivers of the clouds, it's time that we looked at how to use the hybrid clouds in order to maximize the benefits and returns on investments.

We can follow some very simple principles to decide the mix. The following table lists a few samples:

Workloads	Example	Ideal Candidate
Always-on virtual machine	A traditional web/app tier	Private cloud
Unlimited burst ability - short term	Big data workers	Public cloud
Development and test environments	Dev/test environments that will be shut down/destroyed when not in use	Public cloud
Sensitive data	Healthcare (PHI/PII) data, payment (PCI) data	Private cloud
Cognitive services adoption	Next-gen platforms	Public cloud
Rapid prototyping	Any new application where the infra requirements are unknown	Public cloud
Self healing applications	Any application that performs self healing by the integration with monitoring solutions	Public/private cloud

As public clouds become more alike, and with modification of the design principles (moving from IaaS to PaaS), the previous table might change and include a new type of hybrid cloud, which will include multiple public clouds as well.

In the next chapter, we will take a look at the building blocks for mixing both public and private clouds, maximizing the benefits and using the right tool for the job so we don't fall prey to the *law of instrument*.

3
Hybrid Cloud Building Blocks

The fundamental concept of a cloud is the *Lego-block* structure, which means we build what we need. Because of this, there is no single, standard architecture of a hybrid cloud. However, the design principles and methods to build them are available.

This chapter deals with the different building blocks and the principles behind building a hybrid cloud for a variety of use cases, the designs of which range in terms of complexity.

The story of a web application

Before we tackle the different use cases and the building blocks in the rest of the chapter, let's refresh the concepts of how a standard three-tier application would work. If you are wondering as to why this is important, it's because it provides an understanding of the building blocks that we will deal with in the latter part of the chapter.

Most applications found today are *web applications* (applications accessible through a web browser). These range from relatively simple websites such as WordPress, to complicated systems such as Wolfram Alpha. These applications were traditionally 3-tier, comprising of a web-tier, an application-tier, and finally the database-tier.

Now, let's take a look at an enterprise application, such as an employee management system. There are several products on the market, but essentially, it's a system where one would log in to apply for leave, check payslips, and so on. More often than not, this is a web-based system, be it PeopleSoft, an SAP HR module, or a new age SaaS platform such as Workday.

I have chosen the application on purpose, as most of us probably use one at work, it's normally deployed as an internal application (except Workday of course, that's a SaaS), and has role-based access.

Now, you go to a URL that has been provided to you, you sign in, typically using your enterprise credentials, the system logs you in, and shows us the options that we are entitled to.

Behind this simple task of pulling up the website, there are several steps that happen. We will take a look at two aspects of it:

- Transport level
- Application level

Transport level

This section shows the way the connection is created between the browser and the web server. The flowchart shows the process in some detail.

When we start the connection by entering the URL into a browser, the following things happen to create the connection:

1. The browser checks for the presence of a proxy configuration (**Manual** or **Proxy Auto-Configuration** (**PAC**) file).
2. If there is a proxy present, the browser simply submits its request to the proxy and the proxy, after checking its policy, also serves the website back by following through point-3 onwards.
3. If the proxy is *not* present, then the browser requests for the DNS resolution to change the host name into the IP address:
    1. The local cache is checked for the IP.
    2. If the IP is present in the local cache, the TTL value is checked and if the **Time to Live** (**TTL**) has expired, then the DNS query is made to the primary DNS server configured.
    3. If the IP is not present, then the DNS query is also made to the primary DNS server that is configured.
4. Once the IP is found, a TCP connection is made. Default values are port 80 for HTTP, port 443 for HTTPS.
    1. The TCP connection is done by way of the TCP 3-way handshake.
    2. For HTTPS, the TCP handshake is followed by an SSL handshake.
5. Once the connection is successful, the HTTP request is sent to the web server, which then sends an appropriate response back to the system.

The HTTP protocol mainly uses the following reference implementations: HTTP/1.0, HTTP/1.1, and HTTP/2.0. While HTTP 2 support was added to most browsers by the end of 2015, the most used protocol still happens to be HTTP/1.1.

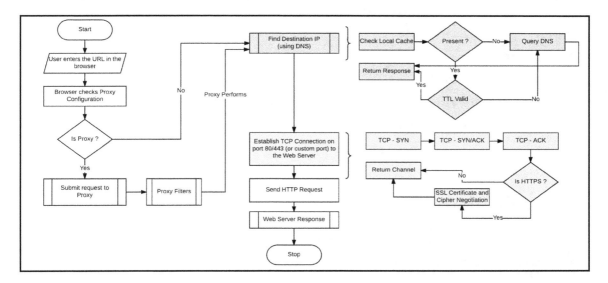

Optional:

To understand this better, the following example emulates connecting to www.google.com and requesting the / (index) page, with and without a proxy. This can be done from any terminal (Command Prompt in Windows and terminal/ssh in Linux or macOS). You should ensure that the telnet client is installed as that will allow us to emulate a TCP connection without having to write our own socket program.

 The following commands are also used to test the connectivity to the website, and may prove useful in troubleshooting the applications, regardless of where it is hosted.

Case 1 – without a proxy

So, we use nslookup to find the IP address of google.com and then use telnet (to start a TCP session on port 80). If we had used the hostname directly in the telnet command, the DNS lookup would have happened in the backend.

Once the connection is established, (it shows the escape character), we make the HTTP GET request as shown using HTTP/1.1 and the web server responds with a new location to follow or a redirect:

```
Aloks-MacBook-Pro:~ alokas$ nslookup google.com
Server:         192.168.1.1
Address:        192.168.1.1#53

Non-authoritative answer:
Name:   google.com
Address: 172.217.27.206

Aloks-MacBook-Pro:~ alokas$ telnet 172.217.27.206 80
Trying 172.217.27.206...
Connected to bom07s15-in-f14.1e100.net.
Escape character is '^]'.
GET / HTTP/1.1
Host: www.google.com
Connection: Close

HTTP/1.1 302 Found
Cache-Control: private
Content-Type: text/html; charset=UTF-8
Referrer-Policy: no-referrer
Location: http://www.google.co.in/?gfe_rd=cr&dcr=0&ei=qvDbWa_YKbCcX7aTl8AH
Content-Length: 269
Date: Mon, 09 Oct 2017 21:56:58 GMT
Connection: close

<HTML><HEAD><meta http-equiv="content-type" content="text/html;charset=utf-8">
<TITLE>302 Moved</TITLE></HEAD><BODY>
<H1>302 Moved</H1>
The document has moved
<A HREF="http://www.google.co.in/?gfe_rd=cr&amp;dcr=0&amp;ei=qvDbWa_YKbCcX7aTl8AH">here</A>.
</BODY></HTML>
Connection closed by foreign host.
```

Case 2 – with a proxy

When we make the request with a proxy, the browser only connects to the proxy and not the actual website. So, the difference in the commands is as follows:

```
telnet <Proxy IP> <Proxy Port>
GET http://www.google.com/ HTTP/1.1
Host: www.google.com
Connection: Close
```

As we can see, instead of sending only the / as a parameter to the GET, we send the full URL, so that the proxy server can make the request on our behalf.

> This will work for HTTP (unencrypted), however for HTTPS the telnet utility shouldn't be used for testing, the openssl command should be used.
>
> A sample of the HTTPS connection is shown as follows (provided openssl is installed on your terminal).

> We will use the s_client or the secure client in the OpenSSL library. The command is shown as follows (used instead of telnet <ip> <port> shown in the preceding example):
> **openssl s_client -connect www.google.com:443.**
> This will then establish a secure channel to the server (by agreeing on the cipher, verifying the certificate, and changing the cipher spec). Once it is done, you can continue to use the HTTP commands as before (GET, Host, Connection, and so on).

Application level

Having understood how we connect from the client (browser) to the web server component of the three-tier architecture, let's take a look at the application level briefly to understand the roles of the different tiers.

Web tier

The web tier normally hosts the static pages and assets required by the application. This includes the HTML files, the CSS, the images, and any other static content. The web tier by its nature should be stateless and hence can be horizontally expanded.

The web tier is implemented by an application, such as Apache, NGINX, IIS, and so on. We normally see that with high volume websites, we may choose to add a cache (memcached or similar) to further enhance the user experience.

Application tier

This tier normally deals with business logic and any computation that may be required. Some persistence is required at this level as the computations might need older references. An example of an application tier would be JBOSS, TomCat, IIS Application Pools, and so on.

 You might have already realized that the IIS application in Windows collapses the web and application tier.

Some example of functions performed by the application tier could be logging in to the application, encoding videos, processing payments, and so on.

It is now almost standard that the application layer's input is the API layer, so the web is decoupled from this layer.

Database tier

This tier is simply used for persistent storage of data. This tier is highly sensitive and requires care to ensure there are no data duplicates when using semaphores or locks. This tier is not something one can rip/replace at will and is dealt with differently.

Putting it all together

Having understood the different components, let's put them together. A sample flow would look something like the following. So, the web tier will serve the HTML, CSS, JS files, images, and other content. The application layer should execute the business logic, and the database layer should store any persistent data:

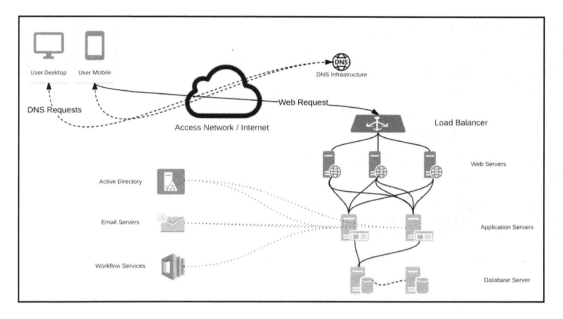

The preceding diagram simply serves to explain that *only* the top tier is actually seen by the user and the remaining tiers are hidden underneath. You may also note that the different tiers are on different network segments.

Armed with this knowledge, let us take a look at the different use cases for the hybrid cloud.

Use cases of a hybrid cloud

We can categorize the use cases broadly into three, based on the existence of different tiers of applications in the clouds, and also the different applications in an enterprise:

- Isolated use cases
- Distributed use cases
- Coexisting use cases
- Supporting application use cases

Isolated use case

This is one of the simplest use cases. In this, an enterprise runs some applications in a public cloud and others in a private cloud, the applications don't communicate among themselves regularly, but may transfer data using a batch process.

It might also be the case that one application uses the services of the other - with the communication over an API.

A good use case in this category would be development in public/production on a private cloud (or vice versa).

In the following diagram, the left side is the public cloud and the right side is the private cloud. The applications running on both sides are isolated - which means a nominal delay in the communication path is acceptable:

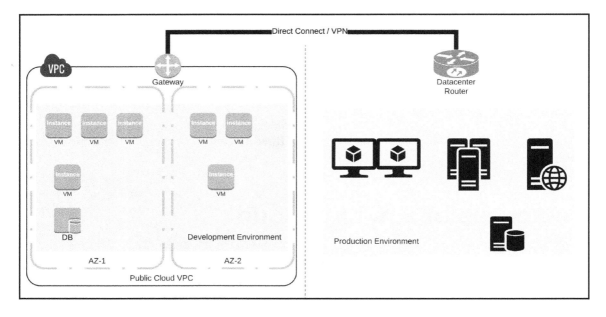

In the preceding example, the environments are completely separated and the compiled/tested code and data may only be moved between the environments manually, or by using a continuous deployment process.

Now, one can choose to keep the development or the production environment in a cloud. Let us look at the rationale behind two use cases:

Requirement	Cloud Type
Data protection standards dictate that data cannot leave the country and the chosen Public cloud doesn't have a region / datacenter in that country	Private
The workload is *bursty* in nature and not always on	Public

Based on this, we can say that dev/test would be a good fit for the public side of the hybrid cloud, while the production system with the production data can sit inside the private cloud/data center as shown previously.

Distributed use case

This one is mainly used with core infrastructure services or the like, where an instance of the application can run on the public cloud and another instance of the same application can be in-house/private cloud.

As an example, take the case of Active Directory. We could have the secondary AD on the public cloud, which will start serving the applications in the public cloud, however they remain in-sync and the public cloud is treated as another *site* in the Active Directory Sites and Services.

Co-Existent use case

This is the most complicated of the three, where some parts of the same application are on the public cloud, while the other parts might be on the private cloud. There are mainly the following motivations that will have you create this kind of an architecture:

- Cloud bursting
- Use of cognitive services from a public cloud
- Licensing restrictions
- Non availability of a service on the Public cloud

You may be wondering, if these are the application's needs, why not move the whole application to the public cloud? The reasons (one or a combination) would be the same as discussed in *Chapter 2, Hybrid Cloud – Why Does It Matter?*, and are noted here simply to refresh your memory:

- Cost of running an application perennially in the public cloud might be higher
- Compliance/security reasons

 If the applications need to use the *co-exist* model, then they need to be architected appropriately. We will look at the application architecture principles a little later in the chapter.

Cloud bursting

Cloud bursting as a concept has been spoken of since the inception of the public cloud. Let's take a simple example to elucidate the need for cloud bursting. Say you run an electronic commerce site and on a festive day or when there is a sale, you get huge bursts of traffic for an otherwise, predictable traffic website.

In this case, one would design the environment to serve the predictable traffic and use the public cloud in order to take over the extra connections.

A few points to note while designing an environment capable of bursting are:

- Stateless and horizontally scalable tier
- Network connectivity and redirection

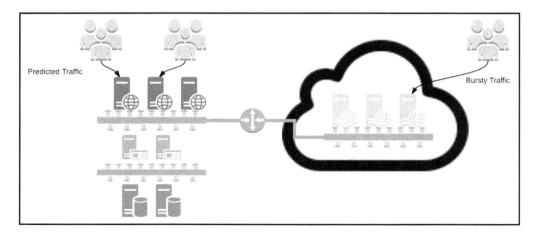

In the preceding diagram, we can see that the **Predicted Traffic** is handled by the application components in the private cloud, however the **Bursty Traffic** is handled by a part of the application that is spun off in the public cloud.

 While in theory, any tier can be bursted, normally only the web or the application tier (or a combination of the two) are considered for bursting in the real world.

If the application is designed appropriately, the scalability of the application can be near infinite with the public cloud being used only for the period of the burst, and the only prerequisite would be having network connectivity in place.

While it is not shown in the preceding diagram, in some cases, some data also needs to be copied between the data center and the public cloud for the tier to work.

Using cognitive services

This is similar in architecture to the connectivity aspect, with the small difference being that the application complements its abilities by using the cognitive services of the cloud.

In order to elucidate, let us consider you are creating a survey application and you want to perform sentiment analysis of feedback submitted to the application via a simple web frontend.

Now, to write a full fledged sentiment analysis application is no easy feat, so you decide to outsource this to the public cloud, say *Google* in this instance. This will be an example of using the public cloud for only the cognitive features.

 In order to use the cloud for just one or two cognitive features, we may not need an elaborate setup, as we might simply be able to connect to the public endpoints and complete the task at hand.

The following architecture might help reinforce our understanding:

As we can see in the previous diagram, the application server is simply making API calls to the endpoints of a few public cloud services and augmenting its capabilities multi-fold.

In these cases, even a private network is not required as these could be accessed securely (using HTTPs) over the internet and also through the enterprise proxies, with little to no modification. What also should be noted is the fact that it is pay per use, so we don't end up paying anything if certain features in the software are not getting used.

Supporting application use cases

This is another kind of use case, where the application is not in the cloud, but its support system is. A good example for this would be backup/disaster recovery in the public cloud, whereas the application itself resides on-premises, in a virtualized environment or a private cloud.

Backup and disaster recovery in the cloud

This is an easy one to implement and only needs network connectivity between the two environments and a software/appliance that can act like a storage gateway enabling tiered storage. This is becoming possible because of the fact network connectivity is growing in terms of speed and reducing in terms of cost.

You might not know it, but you might already be a user of this case as a consumer. Take into account *Google Drive* backup for photos or *iCloud* from Apple. Both of these are standard examples of using the public cloud for the backup of the application, which in this case is the local data store on a mobile phone.

For enterprises, the same principles apply, albeit a little differently. Most tiered storage providers now offer a public cloud as a tier (for archiving), and they would do it on VPN/MPLS links, rather than just sending the data over plain internet.

AWS offers services such as Storage Gateway, S3, and Glacier, targeted towards this requirement specifically. Azure has services such as Azure Site Recovery (ASR) and there are several third-party solutions available to solving this use case.

Decoupling the tiers

We know that the application architecture plays a key role to ensure its candidature for Hybrid Cloud and it should be conducive for the use in some of the use cases.

The first thing that we need to do is to decouple the tiers of the applications if it needs to be considered for distributed or the co-existant use cases mentioned in the afore section. Lets take a look at how is it done:

The two major methods used in decoupling the different tiers are:

- Load balancers
- Queues (AMQP - Asynchronous Message Queuing Protocol)/ESB (Enterprise Service Bus) - (in older applications)

Load balancers are normally used when there is a direct call being made to the tier, this could be the user making a call to the web tier or even the web tier making API calls to the application tier.

An AMQP is normally used when there is a task at hand, and there might be several workers who can pick the task up and do it.

So, in order to understand this better, the use of a load balancer is more of a *Managerial* assignment, where the task is given to the manager, and the manager assigns it to one of the workers, depending upon which one is available and has less work, or even randomly in a round-robin fashion. We would call this a *push* assignment.

We also need to remember that if the worker goes on a long leave, the work may not be completed and the client has to re-request it. The manager would then have to assign it to someone that is available. Also, the manager is completely in grained in the work, which means it is constantly waiting for the work to come back in order to respond.

 A worker in this context is a node or virtual machine in the particular tier that is supposed to service the request being sent to it.

On the other hand, a queue may be used, where the task is kept in the queue and the workers pick it up at their convenience. Once they complete it, they mark it completed. This is a more *social* way to assign work. If the worker dies during the process of finishing the activity, a timer can force the work to be reassigned. The queue is **asynchronous** and normally a call back is made when the work is completed.

The following table explains the differences in short:

Load balancer	Queue
Managerial/push allocation of tasks	Social/pull allocation of tasks
The new worker must register itself with the load balancer when it comes up	Any new worker simply needs to know its *capabilities* and the tasks it can perform when it comes up
If the worker dies during the process, normally no reallocation of the work can be done	If a worker dies, mechanisms can be created for reassignment
Other security features such as Proxying/Web - Application Firewalling, and so on can be added on	Additional features can be added only by using different kinds of workers and modifying the order of queue processing
The Load balancers are normally deployed as a highly-available pair of devices	The queues are normally deployed as a highly-available distributed system
Normally used for frontend HTTP/API connections and between the web and application tier.	Normally used in internal tasks of the application tier

Case in point – architecture of OpenStack

The preceding decoupling concepts will become evident when we take a look at the architecture of the OpenStack system. The system flaunts an application architecture that is distributed with excellent scale and robustness.

OpenStack is a combination of several individual projects that come together to perform a certain function. Some of these projects are:

- **Nova**: Compute as a Service (and some basic network features)
- **Swift**: Object Storage as a Service
- **Cinder**: Block Storage as a Service
- **Glance**: Image repository
- **Neutron**: Network as a Service (including security groups, Load Balancer as a Service, VPN as a Service, and so on)
- **Keystone**: Authentication and Authorization
- **Horizon**: Dashboard

There are several others, but I think those are good enough to make our point. Say we request a virtual machine through horizon after authenticating through Keystone, then Nova will boot the compute after requesting the image from Glance, which will in turn serve the image stored in Swift. After booting, Nova will request the neutron for networking, and may add a persistent volume served by Cinder.

Confused? Don't worry, all we need to know right now is that all of this works together as a well-oiled machine, even after each of these projects are coded by different isolated teams, and it's only the magic of the architecture that makes it work.

Each of the projects have services in them. As an example, there are (Project Name)-api service, scheduler service, and so on. The naming at this level is not consistent, as each and every project may need a different set of services.

The intra-project communication happens in a queue, while inter-project communication happens using the API (which means you can put a **Load Balancer** in front of it). The following diagram shows a small part of the overall architecture, but this design principle is used throughout all the projects:

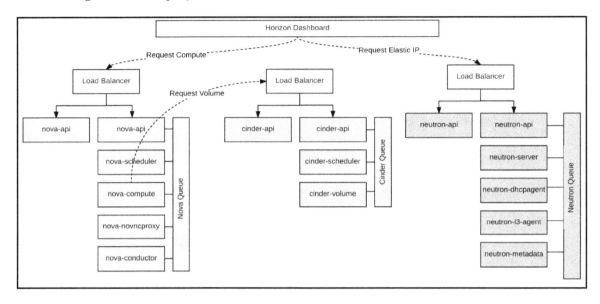

As you can see, now we can simply increase the number of schedulers, conductors, and so on, and no changes need to be made, as their configuration will point them to their queue.

In the event we add new API nodes, we will need to tell the load balancer about it so that all the nodes can get the traffic.

Also, now all of these projects are part of the application (equivalent) tier in the OpenStack's n-tier architecture, they can be put on various machines and it will work just fine.

So hypothetically, a part of the application layer can now reside on a completely different cloud, with only network connectivity.

 Because of the distributed architecture of OpenStack, a company called **Platform9** (https://platform9.com) has created a SaaS offering of OpenStack, which means they host the control plane of OpenStack and the actual virtual machines are spun up in the customer's data center.

Services to enable a hybrid cloud

From all the preceding use cases and explanations, I am sure you have come to the conclusion that there are two major services that are absolutely required to be set up before hand, in order to use a hybrid cloud:

- Network connectivity
- DNS service

A close third would be the core services such as Active Directory, Proxy, and so on but even they will need the preceding, two services so therefore, let's take a look at how these are configured.

Network connectivity

The **network connectivity** forms the backbone of IT and not just the hybrid cloud, so getting this right is of paramount importance. In the case of connectivity between enterprises and the public cloud, the following is a list of requirements that one would need to consider:

- Security of the connection
- Latency
- Bandwidth

So, we cannot do without security, while the levels of the other two depend on the requirements themselves. As an example, if we need to run a voice/video application, then the latency (and jitter) become important. If we are transferring large amounts of data, then the bandwidth needs to be higher.

But based on security, we can infer that we cannot use a vanilla internet connection. So what are our choices?

- IPSec VPN
- MPLS connectivity

We would go for IPSec connectivity in the following cases:

- Amount of data transferred is small
- Low latency requirement is not very high

This normally happens in cases where the footprint of usage in the public cloud is small, and not a lot of data is being transferred, as the environments are more or less isolated.

The MPLS connectivity to a public cloud is normally offered as a service by the public cloud and the ISP. It's known by different names, such as Direct Connect in the case of AWS, Express Route in terms of Microsoft Azure, and Cloud Interconnect in the case of the Google Cloud platform.

While these are provided as a 1 Gbps/10 Gbps connection, several ISPs also provide a sub-1 Gbps connection as determined by the cloud provider service.

The routing normally happens as a static route, for IPSec tunnels and EBGP routing when it comes to MPLS. Please remember that this is simply the most prevalent routing method, and there is no technical reason for it to be as such, however the MPLS connection is definitely recommended to be run with BGP.

DNS service

The **DNS service** also plays a key role in sending traffic to the appropriate servers. This is normally achieved by using the global traffic manager or a global load balancer, which basically combines the concepts of a load balancer and DNS server.

Let's take a quick look at how it works. The global load balancer gets a DNS query for a server record it manages. It then takes a look at the load and availability of the server and then sends the DNS response appropriately.

One thing to remember is that the DNS is only queried (after querying it once) when the **Time to Live** (TTL) expires, hence in order to ensure that the DNS server is queried, we need to lower the TTL. However, as a consequence, the cache is not used for the DNS and there will be a few milliseconds of delay.

Some public cloud like GCP's DNS services provide global load balancing, but other DNS service providers such as Neustar also provide the service. There are enterprise options such as using F5's Global Traffic Manager that can also be used for this feature.

Public cloud services for hybrid deployment

Service providers realized that there was a genuine need for the hybrid cloud, and hence they have designed several services in order to enable this. Let's take a look at these services and the use cases that they can be used to solve.

Amazon Web Services (AWS)

AWS, the original pioneer in the public cloud, has services that can be used for several, previously mentioned use cases of the hybrid cloud. Let's take a look at some of them and the potential use cases where they could play out.

Storage gateway

This service enables hybrid cloud storage. It includes an appliance that can work as a virtual tape library or a file share, which enables tiered storage to be used on the data center/remote office side of things.

Use-Cases: Backup/DR on the cloud, cloud bursting.

Direct connect

This service provides a fast private link into the AWS region using MPLS technology through your network provider. This is one of the most used services from the perspective of the enterprise that has a sizeable footprint in the public cloud.

Use-Cases: All hybrid cloud use cases.

Route 53

This is a DNS service from AWS, which can also perform global load balancing. This is useful in cases such as cloud bursting, Invoking DR, and so on.

Amazon EC2 run command

This is an offbeat service that can be used to manage virtual machines both on-premises and in the cloud. While this is not really required for the functioning of a hybrid cloud, it does play a big role in the operations of a hybrid cloud.

Use-Cases: Operations in a hybrid cloud (not covered previously).

VMware cloud on AWS

The VMware partnership with AWS gave rise to this service. Simply put, we can now run a ESXi, VSAN, and even NSX on bare-metal in the AWS cloud, which allows us to run a VMware private cloud and also a VMware public cloud (in AWS). This could be put to use in various use cases. The details of the service can be found at `https://aws.amazon.com/vmware/`

As an example, you can have a vRealize suite on-premises and add AWS (with the VMware) to make the public cloud look like an additional data center, while being able to use the same orchestration. This service along with vRealize suite, will somewhat rival the AzureStack, albeit in an infra-up mode and not in service down mode.

Microsoft Azure

Microsoft Azure has its own set of services for a hybrid cloud that are different from AWS.

Azure Stack

This is a combination of hardware and software stacks that allow Azure to run on-premises, and can be controlled by the Azure portal in the public cloud. In essence, it allows you to add your personal *data center* to the Azure public cloud visible only to you.

This is by far one of the most comprehensive hybrid cloud solutions out there, however it necessitates the use of certain hardware in a certain reference architecture for you to be able to use it.

Azure Site Recovery (ASR)

This service allows us to have the DR on the public cloud by constantly replicating the on-premises VMs in the Azure Cloud. There is also an Azure Backup service that backs up your servers in the cloud.

Use-Cases: Backup/DR on the cloud.

Azure Traffic Manager

This service, in essence, is a global load balancer and it works in tandem with the ASR. It helps re-point the DNS in the event of cloud bursting or invoking the DR. The Azure traffic manager can work with Azure and non-Azure resources.

Summary – setting up hybrid cloud

I hope that you have understood the building blocks of the hybrid cloud. We now know that the first step in deploying a hybrid cloud is the architecture and configuration of the underpinning services such as network, DNS, and infrastructure core services.

For use cases that are more passive - such as DR and backup services, since it's a one time setup, the setup is done manually. However, for use cases such as creating isolated environments or cloud bursting, an orchestrator is normally used.

One type is the orchestrator, which is used to simply provision the virtual machines and services in both the private and the public cloud. This can be used for the isolated use case.

The other type of orchestrator extends between the clouds and performs infrastructure plumbing in order to perform cloud bursting.

In the remainder of the book, we will be building an example of both of the types mentioned previously. One will be built using a cloud management platform, Scalr, and the other will be built with Kubernetes and Docker.

4
Architecting the Underpinning Services

We have discussed the theory behind several aspects of the hybrid cloud at length. This is the last chapter before we go into full blown implementation mode. In this chapter, we will learn a few details about the basic building blocks before we move on to setting up a cloud management platform and the orchestrated container engine.

It was fairly clear that a network is essential to the hybrid cloud so therefore, that's where we will start. As we progress through the chapter we will take a look at services such as DNS and Identity and Access Management.

While each of the topics described in the chapter deserve a book or more on their own, we are simply looking at the concepts of these systems and at the end, we will architect these services for our hybrid cloud.

Networking

If you are not a network engineer, chances are you have not paid attention to networks other than setting up an IPv4 or IPv6 address. That is because the subject itself is too vast, and most times it just works.

If you have seen people not attempting, or attempting and failing, to build a hybrid cloud, it is because this aspect of it was not heeded to. While networks cannot be learnt in a chapter, we will deal with understanding the aspects essential to the functioning of the hybrid cloud.

We will also introduce some new terms, which we will continue to use in the remainder of the book. However, if you are well versed in networking, you may simply glance over this section.

Underlay network

Simply put, this is the physical network created by using the networking devices, such as switches, repeaters, routers, and some parameter security devices such as firewalls and so on. This includes the medium on which the packets travel by using electrical, wireless, or optical pulses.

The underlay network will only be called as such when the concept of overlay networks enter the picture. Till such a time, the underlay network is simply referred to as the network. So if you hear the word network, it simply means the underlay network.

In the cloud, not a lot is done on the underlay network (except in some private clouds, where the orchestration of this layer is also included) in the design.

LAN architecture

Most people use the Cisco Campus reference architecture (three-tier architecture), or a variation, to implement the LAN of an underlay network. So traditionally, a standard data center architecture may include a core switch/router, a distribution layer, and finally an access layer. Access layers are for connecting end users and servers. The distribution and core layers help in dividing the LAN into smaller chunks by using the VLANs, then connect them using trunks such as **dot1q** trunks.

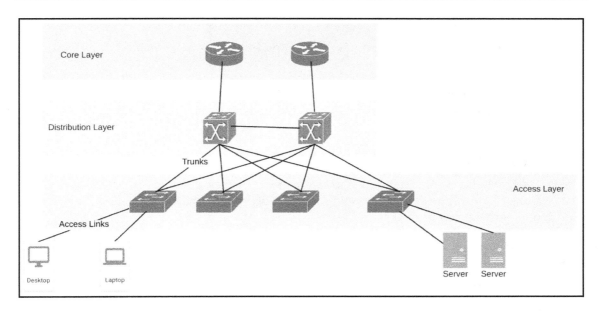

However, with the advent of more powerful switches, the switching architecture has now changed to a collapsed core architecture and sometimes even a fabric architecture (leaf-spine) with Cisco Nexus and Junipers QFabric leading the way.

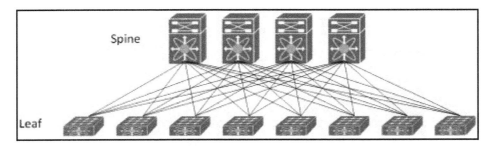

In your data center, you will find either of the previously mentioned topologies or a variation there of.

The orchestration of this layer (if any) would include

- Creating a new VLAN and a new IP subnet for the VLAN
- Creating an SVI (Switched Virtual Interface) to act as default gateway for the IP subnet

- Enabling trunking for the new VLAN.
- Optionally, the deletion of the VLAN and modification to an already existing VLAN

It is to be noted, that normally these things are done on the overlay network, but with the advent of smarter and programmable devices, the underlay may soon be used.

WAN architecture

The WAN architecture, normally used to interconnect offices, is mainly implemented using a hub-spoke or a full/partial mesh topology. While other topologies do exist, in the real world, one of these two is used.

However, we are discussing the logical topology, and this might be implemented by using private links, MPLS, or even an internet connection.

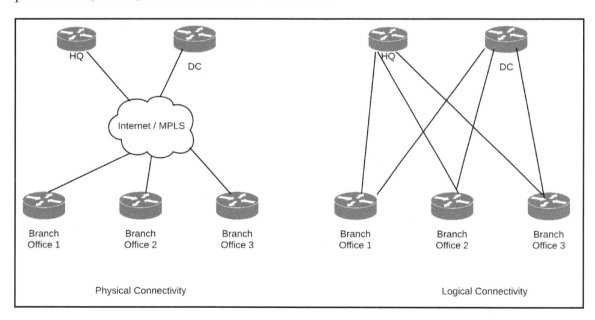

The preceding diagram shows how the physical and the logical connectivity might be created for the connection between the different offices. It is an example of the hub-spoke topology, which means if **Branch Office 1** has to talk to **Branch Office 2**, it will have to go through one of the hub routers.

We will take a look at MPLS and VPNs in a later part of the chapter.

The orchestration of this layer (if any) would be, advertising a new route, and possibly opening a pinhole (allowing access through a firewall for an application) in the perimeter security devices.

Overlay networking

This is the most important part of the cloud ecosystem. These are secondary networks that run over the underlay network in a transparent manner.

 The reason for the existence of the overlay network is the diversity and uncommon programming/configuration standard of the underlay. If a technology such as OpenFlow is implemented and available, then the overlay network may not be needed and both of them might collapse into one.

The overlay network is implemented by using two major technologies:

- GRE - Generic Routing Encapsulation
- VLAN and VxLAN- Virtual LAN and Virtual Extensible LAN

While GREs have been implemented for a long time on physical routers and switches on the WAN side of the overlay to create the required logical topology on the physical links, on the LAN/data center side of the network, these networks are mainly implemented using virtual network devices - such as virtual switches in the hypervisor.

Let's take a look at the technologies before we discuss their usage in a hybrid cloud scenario.

GRE

GRE stands for **Generic Routing Encapsulation** and it is possibly one of the first overlay technologies to be created. Originally, it was created to standardize the layer 4 and layer 3 protocols.

Early in the 1990s, there were several stacks available, for example, TCP/IP, SPX/IPX (from Novell), and Apple talk, among several others. This was a time when ISPs decided to standardize to ensure interoperability.

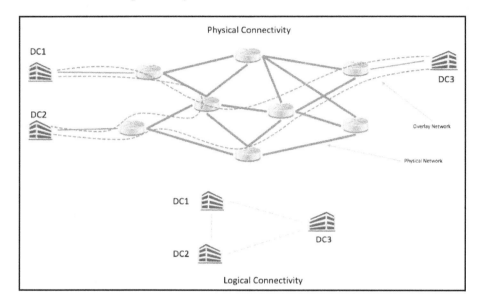

The individual data centers could be using any protocol, the physical network will not get impacted or even see those packets, as they will get encapsulated using the GRE protocol.

Let's take a look at the configuration done on the Cisco device in order to understand the components of a GRE tunnel.

A GRE tunnel will need an address for itself (in this case, the `10.1.1.0/30` subnet is used), the routable IP address of itself (the tunnel source), and the routable address of the destination:

```
Router A#
configure terminal
!
interface tunnel1
ip address 10.1.1.1 255.255.255.252
tunnel source 1.2.3.4
tunnel destination 2.3.4.5
!
```

The other side of the tunnel will then decapsulate the packet and route it appropriately. A similar configuration can be done on Linux boxes as well. (The following configuration is the peer configuration of what is shown previously):

```
Server C#
sudo ip tunnel add gre0 mode gre remote 1.2.3.4 local 2.3.4.5 ttl 255
sudo ip link set gre0 up
sudo ip addr add 10.1.1.2/30 dev gre0
```

Also, since GRE is a standard protocol, we can use the protocol between dissimilar devices. Let us now discuss the encapsulation and decapsulation process:

- Router A encapsulates the packet using the IP address of the physical link IP connecting to router B and tunnel destination IP of the IP address of server C.
- Router B doesn't see the data. Please bear in mind that the data is *not* encrypted, it simply routes the packet as a packet from router A to C. It doesn't care what the payload or the data in the packet is.

 If we wish to encrypt the data inside the tunnel, we can use the IPSec protocol over GRE.

Another form of GRE, called the MGRE or multi-point GRE, has evolved over the last few years to help with multi-point tunnel requirements. This is used alongside with MPLS especially.

VXLAN

Virtual Extensible LAN (**VXLAN**) is an advancement of the VLAN technology itself. Like VLAN, VXLAN is a layer 2 shim, however the major improvements over VLAN are:

- **Number of VXLANs**: Theoretically, this has been beefed up to 16 million VXLANs in a network, thereby giving ample room for growth. However, the devices may support up to 16 or 32 thousand VXLANs. In VLAN, the theoretical maximum was 4,096 VLANs.
- **VTEP**: VXLAN also supports **Virtual Tunnel Endpoint** (**VTEP**), which can be used to create a layer 2 overlay network atop the layer 3 endpoints.

The VXLAN, along with its **VTEP**, are used in proprietary protocols such as **OTV** in Cisco Nexus devices to create stretched layer 2 networks across data centers.

Virtual Private Network (VPN)

The VPN, like most other things in this book can be defined in multiple ways. In essence, it is a private connection to a data center over a shared connection.

This shared connection could be via the internet, the switched network of the ISP (Frame-Relay/ATM), or even a VRF (Virtual Routing and Forwarding) in an MPLS context.

So, how is it achieved? In order to understand this, we need to understand that there are two things to look at:

- The data connection
- The routing table

The first one is fairly straightforward. We don't want other people to see the data that we transmit. This is done by encrypting the traffic using IPSec or SSL. The routing information (the route table) is kept separate by running a routing protocol on the devices at both ends of the tunnel.

However, with the advent of MPLS, the routing information is now shared with the ISP. The ISP, using their VRF (Virtual Routing and Forwarding) configuration, ensure that the integrity of the routing information is kept intact.

So, in short, MPLS takes care of the routing protocol isolation, while IPSec or SSL tunnels can take care of the encryption needs.

 Increasingly, people are not encrypting the data over MPLS connections, as the trust factor on the ISP has grown to ensure that the traffic will not be exposed outside of the assigned VRF. However, there is no technical reason for not being able to do it.

Encrypting data using IPSec and SSL – concepts

The process of encryption is very old, and various methods have been used, such as substitutions, transpositions, and in the modern era, mathematical. However, the science of cryptography is simple. The two parties communicating or intending to communicate need a common code (or a key), with which they can decode the message.

If the same key is used to encrypt and decrypt the message, it's called symmetric key cryptography and if there are two keys involved, it's called public key cryptography.

While these topics are big enough to fill their own books, let's try and understand the concepts, because that is what you would need to do to architect a solution with these things in it.

Given enough time and data, any encryption is breakable.

An encryption is considered broken if the *key* is found by the third-party, so as per the previous statement, we have to continuously keep changing the key, otherwise the encryption will become useless.

So, now we have a second problem, how do we communicate the key without compromising it? A simple answer to this is *Out of Band*. It simply means sending the key in another way. It's similar to receiving our credit/debit card and its PINs separately, or our **one-time passwords** (**OTPs**) being sent using text messaging.

Now, since we have to do this for two devices connected on the network, this becomes a little difficult. Both IPSec and SSL solve this problem for us by using a two-step encryption, let's take a look at how it would work.

IPSec VPN

IPSec, short for **Internet Protocol Security** has become the de-facto standard of encryption on network devices. Before SSL came along, this was used to secure, not only site-to-site connections, but also client-to-site connections.

If you search the internet on how it works, you will come across hundreds or thousands of articles, and I don't intend to add to them. You will hear that there are two phases of IPSec, unimaginatively named, Phase-1 and Phase-2.

You will also understand that there are two protocols at play, the **Internet Key Exchange** (**IKE**) and the IPSec protocol itself. You will find that both phases will be configured with an encryption algorithm, the hashing, the Diffie-Helman group, and so on.

You may be wondering, why two phases? Remember the tunnel inside the tunnel diagram from several blogs. Let me simplify it and remind you of the need for this protocol:

- Data needs to be encrypted and decrypted at the ends so you need a common key for this
- The key needs to change quickly so you need a way to securely transmit the key

The second requirement is taken care of by Phase-1 and the first requirement is taken care of by Phase-2.

So, this is how it works. A random *data encryption key* is generated. That key is encrypted in another key (generated using the Diffie-Helman protocol), which is known to both parties and sent. This concludes Phase-1.

Phase-2 uses the *data encryption key* generated by Phase-1 and then encrypts/decrypts the data with the key.

This will become clear once we see the chronology of how the IPSec tunnel is established.

Step 1 – configuration

In the first step, we configure the two peer devices that will communicate using the following information:

1. Pre-shared key/public key for Phase-1.
2. IP address of the peer, Phase-1.
3. Acceptable ciphers for encryption, Phase-1 and Phase-2. There can be more than one so we can support different devices, however the highest
4. The Diffie-Helman group for Phase-1.
5. Interesting traffic - the traffic that needs to be encrypted. This could be all traffic. This can be an access list (in case of a policy-based VPN) or a route (in case of route-based VPN).

A sample configuration from a Juniper SRX device is shown as follows and the configuration components mentioned previously are marked:

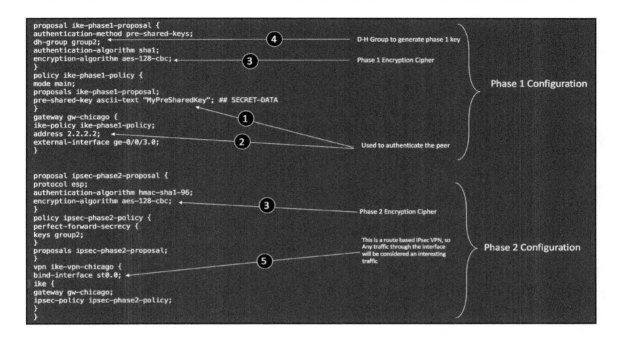

Step 2 – establishing a common data encryption key

In this case, we have device A and device B, who want to communicate. Firstly, they will authenticate each other, by using the pre-shared key for the IP address.

They will then negotiate the encryption algorithms that they will use in Phase 1 from the list of acceptable ciphers.

They then, together generate a *Phase 1 key* using the Diffie-Helman group that is configured. Remember that at *no* time is the Phase-1 key transmitted over the network, the devices compute the same key.

In order to understand how DH works, read through the Wiki article at: https://en.wikipedia.org/wiki/Diffie-Hellman_key_exchange#Cryptographic_explanation

Once the common key is achieved, the device generates the *data encryption key* and then encrypts the key with the *Phase 1 key* and the chosen Phase-1 cipher. The peer device can decode this as it also arrived at the same Phase-1 key using DH. At this point, Phase-1 is considered complete.

Step 3 - encrypting the data

IPSec agrees on the encryption ciphers and using the *data encryption key*, encrypts the data. IPSec keeps changing the data encryption key at a constant interval or whenever the tunnel gets recreated.

SSL VPN

SSL also works on a similar principle as IPSec; the key that is used for the data encryption is generated at runtime, and is encrypted with another key and transmitted.

In this case however, it uses public key cryptography concepts. We need to understand just one concept of how public key cryptography works before we delve into the details of how this would work.

Any data that is encrypted with the Public Key can only be decrypted by Private Key.

SSL VPN, is normally used in a client-to-site (user accessing the data center) situation, but there is no reason we can't use this in the case of site-to-site.

The public key is wrapped in a *certificate*, which is a trusted provider. The server will possess both the public (in form of a certificate) and the private key:

1. Client connects to the server, requests the certificate *(Client Hello)*.
2. Server sends the certificate to the client *(Server Hello, Certificate, Server Hello Done)*.
3. Client authenticates the certificate in the following manner:
    1. It checks the name on the certificate.
    2. It checks if the certificate signer is trusted.
    3. It checks that the certificate has not expired.
4. The client generates a random *data encryption key*.

5. The client encrypts the *data encryption key* with the public key (found in the certificate) and sends it to the server *(Client Key Exchange)*.

6. The server decrypts the *data encryption key* by using its private key.

7. The server and client start to use the *data encryption key* to encrypt and decrypt the data. *(Change Cipher Spec)*.

So, in SSL's case, Phase-1 is replaced by the PKI, which has an added advantage of validating the trust, and means we can start the encryption without having to pre-configure both the client and server. This has been the biggest advantage over IPSec. Imagine if you had to configure the website and your computer for every website you visit. It would be a nightmare.

All the APIs, web services, and other systems are largely protected by SSL, and hence understanding its operation is definitely beneficial. The following screen shows the output of the negotiation of the SSL as captured by Wireshark:

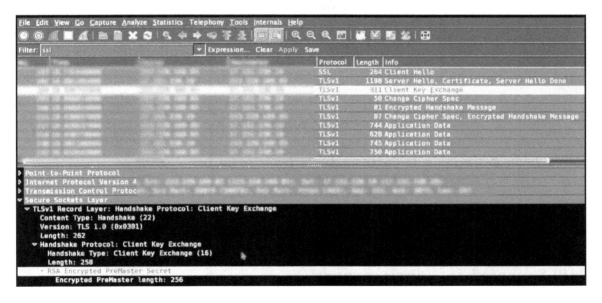

We can also look at the client side by using the openssl client as discussed in the previous chapter. Here is the output (with the certificate truncated, to save space), where the SSL trust chain is being verified:

```
Aloks-MacBook-Pro:~ alokas$ openssl s_client -connect yahoo.com:443          Connecting to yahoo.com on port 443
CONNECTED(00000003)
depth=1 /C=US/O=DigiCert Inc/OU=www.digicert.com/CN=DigiCert SHA2 High Assurance Server CA
verify error:num=20:unable to get local issuer certificate
verify return:0
---
Certificate chain
 0 s:/C=US/ST=CA/L=Sunnyvale/O=Yahoo! Inc./CN=*.www.yahoo.com
   i:/C=US/O=DigiCert Inc/OU=www.digicert.com/CN=DigiCert SHA2 High Assurance Server CA
 1 s:/C=US/O=DigiCert Inc/OU=www.digicert.com/CN=DigiCert SHA2 High Assurance Server CA      Certificate Trust Chain
   i:/C=US/O=DigiCert Inc/OU=www.digicert.com/CN=DigiCert High Assurance EV Root CA
---
Server certificate
-----BEGIN CERTIFICATE-----
MIIJ6zCCCNOgAwIBAgIQDIr8DffyrKO8FF81CMejEzANBgkqhkiG9w0BAQsFADBw
i/CL3Plrq11aJnvVZuNR58dvxg97LwAvK8xb94pVne4xN1mF4yRtGT78JoUwpX2M          Certificate with Public Key (Truncated)
+MjBjAJmctSgmV4wYgkju6vNQD/IsJyh2ZttmeXPhv+inZxgYHgx9H4Dgcf1i7E=
-----END CERTIFICATE-----
subject=/C=US/ST=CA/L=Sunnyvale/O=Yahoo! Inc./CN=*.www.yahoo.com
issuer=/C=US/O=DigiCert Inc/OU=www.digicert.com/CN=DigiCert SHA2 High Assurance Server CA
---
No client certificate CA names sent
---
SSL handshake has read 3920 bytes and written 456 bytes
---
New, TLSv1/SSLv3, Cipher is AES128-SHA
Server public key is 2048 bit
Secure Renegotiation IS supported
Compression: NONE
Expansion: NONE
SSL-Session:
    Protocol  : TLSv1
    Cipher    : AES128-SHA                                                     Cipher and Key Sent
    Session-ID: 7C8AC99BFB496C1C322DAB5DBF816E74B1C07E9B2F20CCBBD9E608953A551DE8
    Session-ID-ctx:
    Master-Key: BD1FA3A89F6054EDE819F6006510E657B0E6DB44E9692193581C7FF92727E32BE23BA1FD3CF477985FFF65286D41A698
    Key-Arg   : None
    Start Time: 1509372779
    Timeout   : 300 (sec)
    Verify return code: 0 (ok)
---
```

So, the previous methods are used in the encryption of the traffic.

MPLS connectivity – direct connect

Public clouds allow us to use MPLS connectivity to a co-location, where the cloud providers have also terminated their inbound service link. Note that this kind of virtual network is not encrypted, but simply isolated using the routing tables (read more about it in the following section).

This kind of service is available from all the major cloud service providers:

- AWS - Direct Connect
- Azure - Express Route
- GCP - Cloud Connect

Routing table

Static routes are used mostly in VPNs, with IGPs, such as OSPF, EIGRP, and so on run between the peers. With the advent of MPLS and the increase in adoption of VRF, where companies peer directly with the service provider, BGP became the most favored protocol.

In order to elucidate this a little further, take a look at the following diagram which shows how the connectivity between two of the sites are using the ISP:

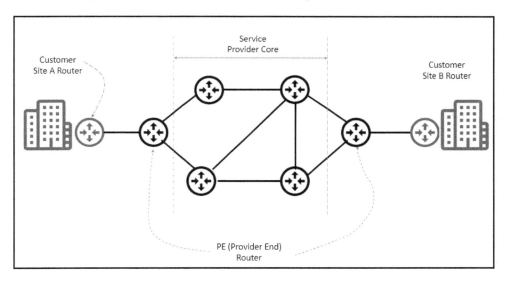

Now, in the case of using an encrypted tunnel (using IPSec) or an non-encrypted overlay (using GRE), the routing table is shared between the two customer routers - either by using static routing or a routing protocol such as OSPF, EIGRP, or even BGP. The ISP routers have no knowledge of the routes that the customer is using.

This is because, in the standard mode, the ISPs can't differentiate between the routes from customer A and customer B, which will be running on the same ISP core. So, the routing would look as follows:

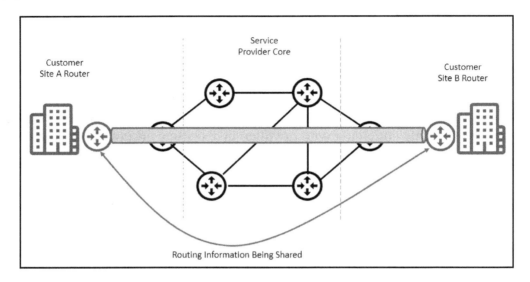

But with **Multi Protocol Label Switching** (**MPLS**), the routing peering is done directly with the ISP, which peers with us using a VRF and then uses the core to optimally route the traffic through the core. (Remember, the traffic is not encrypted in MPLS, and you have to use IPSec/SSL over it if we want to stop the ISP from being able to snoop the traffic).

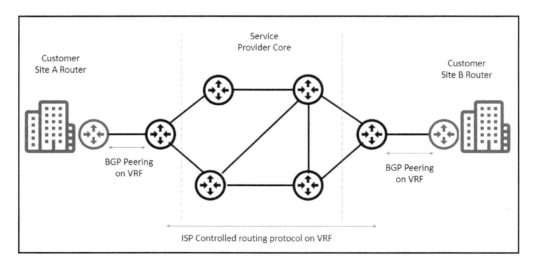

Also, a very simple explanation of VRF is that the service provider routers, in addition to having a global routing table, have smaller virtual routing tables that are associated with end interfaces (in the case of PE routers) and with labels (the "L" of MPLS) in the provider core, so the routes don't mix with routes of other customers.

Understanding this part is essential because most high bandwidth connections to the cloud use MPLS ,and understanding this will help you appreciate the need for BGP configuration while setting up the hybrid cloud.

Domain Name System (DNS)

Having understood the basics of networking, let's take a look at the second important underpinning service, the DNS or the Domain Name System. In the case of the hybrid cloud, it is instrumental to redirect traffic appropriately to the servers from the user machines (or even between the servers).

Before we get into how this works with hybrids, let's quickly understand the basics of the DNS query and how we can manipulate it into sending the traffic to different places.

How does DNS work?

The DNS system, on the most simplest levels, consists of a database that contains different kinds of associations. These associations are called DNS records.

There are several types of DNS records, some of which are mentioned in the following (there are several others out there, but the list should be enough to help us understand):

- **A record**: Association between host name and IPv4 address
- **MX record**: Association between domain name and the IP address of its SMTP server
- **CNAME record**: Association between a name and another name
- **PTR record**: Reverse association - IP address to hostname
- **NS record**: Association between the domain name and the IP address of its DNS server

In order for us to understand a DNS query and its response, (say we want to go to the email server of Google, `mail.google.com`), we need to look up the IP address with the hostname. So we will perform an "A" query, by using a tool such as nslookup or dig:

```
C:\Users\alokas>nslookup
Default Server: google-public-dns-a.google.com
Address: 8.8.8.8

> mail.google.com
Server: google-public-dns-a.google.com
Address: 8.8.8.8

Non-authoritative answer:
Name: mail.google.com
Address: 209.99.64.53
```

So, we got the output, but how did it fetch it? DNS is a very hierarchical system, akin to a postal system. Say you are sending a letter from India to Google's Mountain View campus (1600 Amphitheatre Pkwy, Mountain View, CA 94043, USA), so how would the letter be delivered?

The answer is by following the address backwards. The mailing company will see it needs to go to the USA, then once it reaches there, it will find the way to California, then Mountain View, then Amphitheatre Parkway, and finally to the number 1600.

DNS also works the same way, first it will go the servers responsible for `.com` (called the root hint servers), and then find out how to get to `google.com`. Then they will go to the name servers of `google.com` and ask how to get to `mail.google.com`, and finally give us the output of the A record that we have requested. This can easily be seen by the command, `dig +trace`:

In order to do the trace, you can use `dig +trace <Hostname>` if dig is installed on your system. Alternatively, you can use the web interface and choose *trace* under Options from the website: `https://www.digwebinterface.com/`.

In the output, you will see that the system goes to the root hint server, which provides the NS record for Google's DNS servers, and finally gets to the A record after looking for the `CNAME` record of `mail.google.com`.

It is also important to know that the DNS records come with a TTL. This value is the time for which the response from the DNS can be cached. The lower the time, the faster a DNS change will be made.

Global load balancing

This is normally done by DNS resolution. For example, if I request `mail.google.com` from India, the global load balancer will resolve the IP address of a server which is closer to the region (geolocation), and if the India region goes down, then the DNS will resolve to an alternate site, say the USA.

There are two major ways this is configured:

1. DNS Anycast
2. Geolocation-based DNS

In anycast mode, the DNS requests using BGP for the same IP address to be routed to different DNS servers, which can have different IP addresses. In the second mode, based on the location of the IP address from which the DNS request is being made, the responses can be different.

Now pair this with the DNS server's ability to monitor the availability of the actual server and alter the records dynamically, and you now have a global load balancing system.

We can use this ability to configure hybrid cloud bursts and more. As an example, the first 1000 people can be served with the IP address of your on-premises server. The DNS server can monitor the server's load and once it is high, it simply starts forwarding the newer clients to the IP address of the server on the public cloud.

We could use cloud-based services from pure-play DNS service providers such as Neustar, or even the public cloud service providers, for example, the AWS Route 53 in order to do this.

Identity and Access Management (IAM)

The next underpinning service used is the Identity and Access Management Service. Traditionally, this meant having a common directory which the applications can query to authenticate end users.

The IAM is normally a **team effort** between the system that can store and authenticate the users (the directory), and also provide the ability for us to tag the users and the application in some way. The application uses the tags in order to control the permissions for the user. The ability to fine-tune the authorization is called **Role Based Access Control (RBAC)**.

So, it can safely be assumed that the a*uthentication* is dependent on the directory. The *authorization* on the other hand is dependent on the application, which use the *tags* that are associated to the user or that the user is associated to.

 In the case of Active Directory, the user is added to the "tag", in this case called the "Security Group" and in the application, we would define whether the user belongs to this group and grant/deny a certain access.

Identity Federation

There have been several kinds of user directories and protocols to access these directories, the most common ones are however, Microsoft Active Directory and the LDAP (Lightweight Directory Access Protocol) to access it. Since these directories are a single source of truth in most enterprises, we can't risk them by having them in a single deployment, so they support the distributed architecture by default.

In traditional systems, the applications directly query one of the directory servers, and pull the data they need (member groups, tags, and so on). However, as more and more applications try to authenticate with the central directory, especially applications coming from beyond the controlled network, it becomes difficult and unsafe for us to simply open direct access to the directory.

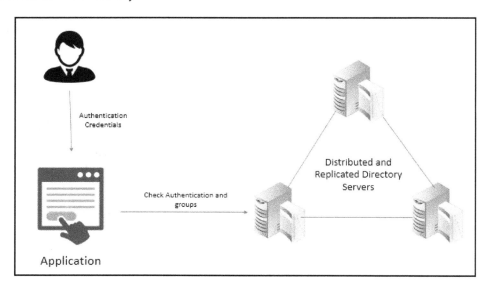

In order to mitigate the risk of opening the directory to third-party applications, people started having different credentials for different applications and this brought its own challenges.

In order to illustrate the problem, let us take a consumer example rather than an enterprise one. Consider the several websites that we use today: Gmail, Facebook, Pinterest, news websites, and so on. Each of them have their own user directories, where your user and password are stored.

Now, you have to remember several different usernames and passwords. Even if you choose to have the same password, when you need to change it you have to manually change it and these websites can't allow direct access to one another for security and scale ability reasons.

The solution? I am sure some use it. Social logins. Several websites allow you to log in to their websites using your Facebook, Google, or OpenID credentials. This concept is called **Single Sign On (SSO)**. Of course, even now, Facebook/Google don't open their directories to the website, but it is achieved through *Identity Federation*.

The main standards that help in identity federation are SAML and OAuth. SAML provides authentication (SSO) and OAuth is purely for authorization. There are several IAM products implemented by these standards and help us in enabling SSO - examples include ADFS, Ocata, and so on.

The SAML standard works with various transport formats such as HTTP (Redirection and Post Binding). It can also be used with other transports such as JMS.

OAuth however, requires HTTP exclusively. So, in the case of identity federation, normally HTTPS is used as it's the common factor.

In order to understand the basics of this, we need to know the following major roles:

- **Identity provider (IdP)**: This is equivalent to your traditional directory front-ended by a web service that can sign tokens
- **Service provider**: This is the application that you are trying to access

So the authentication flow follows the following steps:

1. User requests the web application (service provider).
2. Web application checks the authentication token, since this is the first request it doesn't find it.

3. The service provider then identifies the correct identity provider (based on username - in Azure, the domain name that was accessed, IP address, and so on) and redirects the user using a HTTP 3XX code (normally 302) to the identity provider.
4. The user goes to the identity provider page and enters their credentials.
5. The IdP authenticates the user with the directory in the backend, generates a token, signs the token, and gives it to the user browser.
6. The IdP finally redirects the user back to the service provider.
7. The service provider checks the token (same as the first step), but this time finds the token and allows the user to access the website (based on the local authorization database).

> If you have not already experienced this, open an incognito mode browser, such as Chrome, open the developer tools - by pressing *F12* (or equivalent for your browser). The reason for opening in incognito mode is so that your login credentials in your normal browser instance don't save the history and cookies after we close them.

> Now, you can access any one of the Google-operated website, such as YouTube, Google Maps, Gmail, and so on. For instance, for Gmail, you will see that you get redirected to `accounts.google.com`. In this case, Gmail is the service provider and accounts.google.com is the identity provider.
>
> Once you log in, you can use the same browser session to go to another website in the list, and it will not be required for you to re-authenticate, as the same IdP controls the website.

You can use the developer tools in a browser to inspect the headers being set for the authentication process.

Multi-Factor Authentication (MFA)

While this does not help or impede the hybrid cloud, this simply enhances the authentication process and increases security by using two or more factors (what you have and what you know). It is like using an OTP or a hard/soft token along with a password.

This can simply be considered an enhancement to the already existent directory. Most public cloud services already have the capability to enable MFA in their IAM service.

Application components

Along with the previously mentioned underpinning services, some application components can also be considered underpinning services. In this case, I am talking about the database. Due to it storing persistent data (and the sheer volume of data) and necessity to be consistent, special care should be taken when designing a database for a truly hybrid cloud experience.

There are two modes in which one could operate the database in a cloud scenario:

1. Using global databases
2. Using one of the clouds in the hybrid setup to act as a DR/backup of a traditional database

Again, the mode we would run is completely dependent on the application architecture and what we intend to do with it.

Global databases

While most of you might be familiar with standard RDBMSes (Relational Database Management Systems) such as MySQL, MS-SQL, Oracle, and the like, you might not be aware of No-SQL databases and Graph databases. Let's talk about a new age database we like to call a "Global Database".

Google spearheaded a new type of database that combined the aspects of both traditional RDBMSes and No-SQL databases. The database is called **Google Spanner**. Please see the following for the feature differences between the three:

Feature	Google Spanner	Traditional RDBMS	Traditional No-SQL
Schema supported	Yes	Yes	No
Consistency (all the nodes in the distributed architecture have the same data)	Strong consistency	Strong consistency	Eventual consistency
Availability	High	Failover Only	High

Scalability (Horizontal - Add more nodes to add capacity, Vertical - Add more RAM/CPU/Disk to the same node to add capacity)	Horizontal	Vertical	Horizontal
Replication	Automatic	Manual configuration	Manual configuration

So, one may argue that Google Spanner is the best of both worlds. Google Spanner is an RDBMS system, where you can write the data on any node and read from any node and it will be consistent. An application of this kind is absolutely mind boggling especially when it comes to hybrid cloud.

 The only thing to remember is that data consistency takes a few (1-7) microseconds and should be considered near real-time, which is good for most applications. However, applications need actual real time data. For a stock exchange, where a millisecond delay would cause harm, this database cannot be used.

However the downside is that Google Spanner, at the time of writing this book, is only available for use in the Google Cloud Platform. This means, using it outside the Google Cloud (even for a hybrid cloud solution with GCP) is not possible.

However, the open source community, being eager, has created an open source Google Spanner equivalent called Cockroach DB (https://www.cockroachlabs.com/). If you are wondering about the reason behind the name - it's simple, you can't kill it (not easily at least). Using Cockroach DB, we can get a global DB for our hybrid cloud setup.

 Microsoft Azure launched Cosmos DB, which is similar to Google Spanner and now AWS's Dynamo DB also offers Global DB features.

In a hybrid cloud environment, we can use neither Google Spanner or Cosmos, because they are public cloud-only versions, but Cockroach DB will fit the bill perfectly.

Using Cockroach DB in a hybrid cloud environment

Consider an environment where an e-commerce site is running in hybrid mode as follows. With the global DB, the public cloud instances, or the private cloud/DC instances can work as if it's an isolated environment, and the global database will take care of ensuring the data consistency.

The capability and the extent of functionality of Cockroach DB was shown at the OpenStack summit in Boston 2017. About 15 clouds ran a single distributed cockroach DB instance:
`https://thenewstack.io/openstack-summit-presented-convincing-dem`
`o-cross-cloud-convergence/`

There is a user recorded video of the session can be found here (the video quality is not great): `https://www.youtube.com/watch?v=mPKbUIk_Mxo`

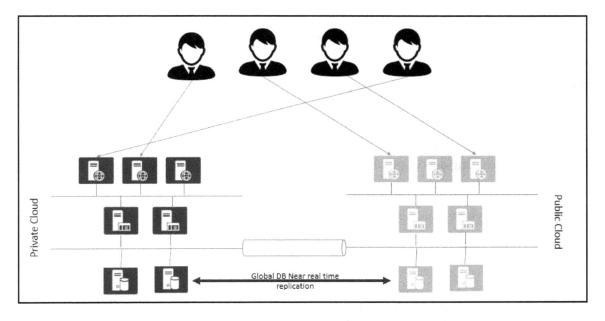

As you can see in the preceding figure, the same application is running at the same time, on both the sides of the hybrid cloud, and the web servers and application servers don't even need to be aware of the existence of the parallel application stack and still work harmoniously.

Database log shipping

Of course, in order to use global databases, you will need to rewrite the application (or some part of it). However, if that is not a feasible solution then sometimes we set up a standard RDBMS with log shipping between the private and public cloud.

Log shipping is possibly one of the most standard ways to create a warm DR environment (or even master-slave) configuration. In this case, the other environment is not active, but can help when failing over due to a DR invocation. We can also simply run it on a high-powered machine in the cloud to handle burst.

Choosing the right components

Having understood the previous concepts, let us take a look at the architectural decisions we would have to take when designing a hybrid cloud. In order to do so, we will ask ourselves some questions and the answers should lead to us choosing the right components.

Network connectivity

In this, we are trying to determine three major things:

- The connectivity aspect
- The routing aspect (somewhat dependent on the connectivity aspect)
- The redundancy aspect

So the questions you would ask are:

1. What kind of hybrid cloud use cases do we envision to use now and in the future?

   This is the same as what was discussed in the last chapter. Are we trying to use the public cloud simply for backup/DR, an isolated environment, or a burst able environment? Don't worry if the answer is all of them.

2. How much traffic is anticipated to pass between the two environments?

   We can ascertain this by taking into account the application architectures and the use cases that were answered in the previous question

3. Are there any jitter/delay sensitive applications?

    This would be a yes if it is a VoIP or video application between the clouds

4. How critical is the hybrid cloud to the business?

    This question is to ascertain what kind of redundancy we are looking at

5. Does the business connectivity already include MPLS connectivity between the site offices and the HQ?

    This question will simply help you evaluate the feasibility of using a Direct Connect kind of link.

6. Is the availability of bandwidth low/expensive?

    While this is not normally a problem these days, this will allow us to decide if we need WAN optimization devices/services. (Some providers provide WAN optimization as an add-on bundle when you take an MPLS circuit from them).

Question #	Answer	Option
1	Large number of use cases	MPLS connectivity (direct connect)
	Less use cases	IPSec VPN over internet links
2	High traffic	MPLS connectivity
	Low traffic	IPSec VPN
3	Yes	MPLS connectivity
	No	IPSec VPN
4	Very critical	Depending on the criticality level, you may run two MPLS links. If the criticality is less, we can use IPSec VPN as the redundant connection.
	Not critical	No need for redundancy or IPSec VPN redundancy
5	Yes	MPLS connectivity
	No	IPSec VPN connectivity

This should help us choose the link. Choosing a routing protocol is possibly easier. If MPLS connectivity is chosen, then BGP routing becomes de-facto, but over IPSec VPN, it's mostly static routing.

DNS services

The list of questions that we would ask ourselves area as follows:

1. Are we going to be using dynamic cloud bursting?

   This will determine if we need global load balancing

2. Are we going to be using the cloud for backup/DR ? If so, RTO (Recovery Time Objective)?

   This will be used to determine the TTL for the DNS records

3. Are the IP addresses for the host names different while accessing the services from inside and outside the enterprise?

   This question is to determine if we need split DNS

    A split DNS is where we have two set of DNS servers; one for internal use and the other for outside access.

   While it might seem a logical thing to do, more and more enterprises on an Internet First policy will send internal users via internet links rather than private links.

Once we have the answers to the questions, we will be able to architect the DNS. Of course, do keep in mind that if Dynamic DNS is required, ensure the platform doing the global load balancing offers an API to be able to programmatically modify the DNS records (or has the ability to monitor the servers).

IAM and Active Directory

This one is simpler to architect. The questions that we need to think about are the following:

- Do third-party systems need authentication or plan to use SaaS?

  If yes, we will need a system that can perform federation, such as ADFS

- Do a lot of internal applications in the public cloud need to access the Active Directory?

  If yes, we will create a secondary domain controller/additional domain controller in the public cloud and add the relevant sites and services information

Of course, other problem statements such as certification authority servers and key management systems will need to be considered along the same lines.

Other services such as databases and other core services such as web proxies and IPS/IDS (intrusion prevention/detection systems) are designed in and almost traditional manner and hence are not discussed here.

Conclusion

In this chapter, we saw the available options, the questions and reasons to choose certain options over others. It is imperative that we pay close attention to this because, the quite literally will form the foundation of the Hybrid Cloud that we intend to build on top of it.

Please ensure that we build the foundation based on what we want our Hybrid Cloud to do when it is completed, and not necessarily based on the immediate goals. In the coming chapters, we will put all of this together and create a Hybrid Cloud with a single pane of glass provisioning and special use cases (storage/DR/backup) on the public cloud.

5
Hybrid Cloud Deployment – Architecture and Preparation

It is finally the time to put all the theory we have learnt into practice, and create an environment that will be used to show the implementation of the different use cases possible in the hybrid cloud.

For this, we will need a private cloud environment and a public cloud environment connected to each other. The private cloud environment will be run from our data center, so, we can also assume that the *traditional* workloads are also there.

In order to set this up, we will use OpenStack as the private cloud and we will create an AWS VPC for a public cloud infrastructure. Since, we are using this as a lab or demo environment, we will simply use the IPSec VPN to connect between the two as no particular jitter-sensitive applications are going to be running in the environment.

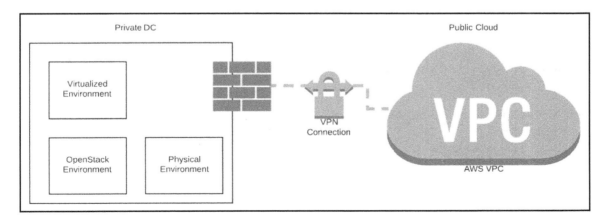

In this chapter, we will also look at the use cases that allow the hybrid cloud to be more *pragmatic* in nature.

 A **hybrid cloud** is said to be pragmatic when one end is the public cloud and the other end is holistic, by including the physical and virtual environments in the private data center in addition to the private cloud.

Getting started with the public cloud – AWS

So, regardless of the fact that we are integrating it with only a private cloud, or being realistic and integrating it just with a virtualized data center, we still need to set up the public cloud. In this case, we have chosen to set up AWS as our public cloud, however, the concepts will be similar for other cloud providers.

AWS is nothing short of a technological marvel. The scale they operate at is just mind-boggling. In order to give you an idea of the scale they operate at, read the following quote:

> *"In 2015, AWS almost deployed enough server capacity EVERYDAY to support Amazon in 2005, when it was an $8.49 Billion Enterprise"*
> *- James Hamilton, VP & Distinguished Engineer, AWS,*
> *(Re:Invent 2016)*

Now, we can assume that enough capacity is being added to support a Fortune 500 company, every day of the year.

To top it off, AWS also uses its own network equipment and its own undersea cables running about 100 waves of 10 GBps each on an optical fiber in full-redundancy.

 If you want to hear the full presentation from James Hamilton, with details on the AWS infrastructure at scale, you could visit: `https://www.youtube.com/watch?v=AyOAjFNPAbA`

Before we start setting up our own little piece of this public cloud, let's understand some of the terminology.

AWS terminology

If you have worked with AWS, you would already know this. However, just to ensure that we are all on the same page, I am mentioning the terminology you need to know to get started with your AWS architecture. Please remember that this is not an exhaustive list.

 If you want to know all the different terminology in use, please refer to the glossary at: `http://docs.aws.amazon.com/general/latest/gr/glos-chap.html#A`.

Account

The easiest way I can explain this is that an **account** is a billing/payment construct. It is quite literally an *account* that is allowed to use AWS services. You need to set an account up before we can spin anything up on AWS. It's normally associated with a credit card, which gets charged at the end of a billing cycle.

For enterprises however, the bill of all accounts can be charged to a master paying account.

Region

A **region** is a geographical tag where AWS resources are located. This is mostly on a city level. For example, North Virginia, Sydney, Mumbai, and so on are regions. Each region comprises multiple Availability Zones. The data transfer out of the regions will typically be carried by some undersea cables, and they are chargeable.

Availability zones (AZ)

An **AZ** is a collection of **one or more** data centers, a region will be made out of a few of them (minimum of two). The data centers in the availability zones are connected with high-speed fiber, with a single digit latency.

Virtual private cloud (VPC)

A **VPC** is a private network that you can create for your own cloud in AWS. In a way, the VPC can be considered your personal network space.

You start out by defining the major subnet, and then divide these into smaller pieces called subnets. VPCs also include gateways to reach the internet or the VPN (called Internet Gateways and VPN gateways respectively).

It is inside these VPCs that you create the resources that are needed. A VPC spans a region, but the subnets span only an AZ.

AWS services

AWS keeps adding services and features to services at such a rapid pace, that it is almost impossible to write about them in a book and expect it to still be relevant. It is for this reason, that I point you to their official website for the list of services that they have currently.

 Refer https://www.amazonaws.cn/en/products/ to see the list of services that the cloud offers (at the time of writing, there were about 100 services being offered).

Let's take a look at some of the services:

Service name	Category	Description
Virtual public cloud (VPC)	Networking	Allows us to create private networking and connectivity in the public cloud
Elastic Cloud Compute (EC2)	Compute	Provides the compute resources (RAM and CPU) for creating a virtual machine and some storage space which is ephemeral in nature.
Elastic Block Storage (EBS)	Storage	Provides persistent block storage (disk) to be attached to an EC2
Load Balancers (ALB / NLB)	Compute	Provides load balancing across multiple EC2 instances
Route 53	DNS	Provides DNS services
Simple Storage Service (S3)	Storage	Provides object storage to safely store BLOB's or Binary Large Objects. These could include anything from human readable files to binary files used by the computers

Like the demographics that we learnt about in the first chapter, it is enough to say that in order to architect an AWS cloud, you would need to know about two types of data:

- **Service category**: This is mentioned in the previous link and includes categories such as compute services, developer services, storage services, and so on
- **Service boundary/scope**: We will discuss this in this section of the book

If you have ever written a program, you would know that there is a *scope* of a variable where said variable will be active.

The AWS services can be divided into:

- **Global services**: The service that acts across all regions
- **Regional services**: The service that acts across all availability zones of a region
- **Zonal services**: The service that is constrained to a single availability zone

 It is to be noted that cloud providers don't have many global services, as they don't want to replicate any data between the zones, mostly for compliance reasons. However, if the customer wishes to replicate the data, that is possible, but we would need to pay the "data-out" fees to get the data from any region (data into a region is free).

Now, most services are zonal in nature, however, let's take the previous list and look at the scope:

Service name	Scope
Route 53	Global
VPC	Regional
ELB	Regional
EC2	Zonal
S3	Regional
EBS	Zonal
Elastic IP	Regional
Subnets	Zonal

In order to understand this, please bear a few things in mind:

- There are few global services, because the customer data is kept within the region
- There is no technical reason for not doing it, but there are compliance reasons
- Anything that cannot move outside a data center is zonal

For example, you can't attach a disk from a data center to another one (which could be a few hundred miles away) for performance reasons. A subnet in your data center can only be extended to another, if we have layer 2 connectivity. That is not a good idea for large distances.

However, the load balancer (NLB/ALB) can load balance between servers in more than one AZ, and that is why it is called a regional service. S3 replicates the objects to five or more copies across multiple AZs to give redundancy, and therefore it's a regional service.

 ALB from AWS has the ability to load balance between the onpremise (Private) and the Public clouds, so it makes a good solution to make a Hybrid Cloud.

Architecting the AWS environment

In this section, let's talk about the first principles in architecting the AWS environment. We have to take a look at the following:

- AWS account design
- AWS VPC design

AWS account design

While a single account is more than sufficient technically, there are reasons why you might want to have several accounts. An account is a level which has *limits* applied, so people choose to have the following:

- Different accounts for different business units

    Helps in separation of usage and billing details

- Different accounts for production and non-production environments

  You may consider this, not only for the separation of usage and billing information, but also for the fact that testing may inadvertently overload a server. The non-production account may face a temporary ban, and if the production servers are on the same account, these servers may face an outage. Also keeping the accounts separate may help in separation of the duties and access can be controlled in the same way.

A combination of the two reasons may also be used (as an example, production for a particular business unit). While using multiple accounts, it's a good idea to have a single payment account, so the billing is consolidated.

VPC design

The **VPC design** is from a networking standpoint. It follows similar principles from a data center perspective. One VPC is created per region. As when designing the networking for a data center, a supernet is created, for example `10.1.0.0/16`, and then this is further divided into smaller/24 subnets.

Normally, one VPC per region is technically sufficient. You may want to consider the following:

- One VPC per department (or group of departments)
- One VPC for a certain kind of applications—for example, a VPC for all the systems that need HIPAA compliance
- Different VPCs for customers and core IT workloads

  Refer to the following links to learn more about AWS VPC:

- http://docs.aws.amazon.com/AmazonVPC/latest/ GettingStartedGuide/getting-started-ipv4.html
- http://docs.aws.amazon.com/AmazonVPC/latest/ PeeringGuide/peering-scenarios.html

In simple terms, the VPC can be considered a Private Network Namespace for a region, in which we can create several subnets (in an AZ). The subnets normally fall into two categories:

- **Public subnet**: Connected to the internet using an Internet gateway.
- **Private subnet**: Isolated from the internet. We can use a Virtual Gateway to connect it to internal networks or our data center. We may also connect the machines to the internet using a proxy.

Designing an AWS environment

Let's take a scenario, and design an environment for it. So, we are designing the AWS environment for a fictitious company, Acme Inc., which is a conglomerate that has five different business units, *Real Estate, Healthcare, Oil, Gas, Transport,* and the *Corporate* unit, which takes care of the remaining four BUs.

Each of the business units are autonomous, however, the corporate IT team takes care of the IT and security requirements for all business units. For the preceding BUs, IT is not a main business, but an enabler. All of them have several COTS, FOSS, and bespoke applications that they want to move to AWS. The bespoke applications have development, testing, and UAT environments.

We need to get the answers to the following questions (and other relevant ones for the design):

1. Does the company have centralized IT billing?
2. For each BU, what percentage of the IT utilization is development and testing?
3. Do we have separate departments that use IT and would want their environments isolated from a network standpoint for security or compliance reasons?
4. Does the common IT security policy allow direct internet access or through a proxy?
5. Are the applications directly exposed to the internet or are they intranet only applications?
6. Do the applications that are being deployed have HA or a multi-AZ environment?

Now, depending on the answers, here are a few guidelines for the design points:

Question no.	Answer	Decision point influence
1	Yes	We will need to create a single *paying* account to which all other accounts will be mapped.
	No	The individual accounts would suffice. While an account doesn't cost anything on its own, there is no harm in creating a common paying account.
2	High/Medium	Considering that we will create an account per BU, we should consider a different account for production and non-production workloads.
	Low	The same account can be used for both production and non-production workloads.
3	Yes	Multiple VPCs will be needed per region per account.
	No	We could use a single VPC per region in an account.
4	Direct access	We can use public subnets with Internet Gateways (IGW) in the VPC.
	Proxy access	We should have a private subnet for the workloads, we may have a public subnet where the proxy can sit.
	Both - depending on application	Multiple subnets of both types are required in a VPC.
5	Yes - direct internet access	Public subnets with elastic IP address and/or frontend by NLB/ALB. The best practice is to use the Load balancing service to front end the public subnets
	Intranet only	Private subnets connected to the data center by VPN/direct connect is used.
6	Single-AZ	Subnets are only created in the single availability zone.
	Multi-AZ	This is actually a best practice, and subnets need to be created in two or more availability zones.

Do remember that these are simply references that you can use in the design, and the final design should be implemented by also considering the applications that we need to run in the public cloud.

Availability zones are created on different flood planes, and so it's a best practice to at least design the subnets for two AZs, if not three (where possible), even if there are no current applications to utilize them.

If the said design is not done as mentioned previously, we may be able to add these later into the VPC.

The support services in AWS, such as accounts, VPC, subnets, and so on are free and so a design should incorporate best practices, keeping the future in mind rather than just designing for today.

That being said, coming back to our Acme Inc. use case, let's design it. It's clear that the best way to do it will be by creating different accounts for different BUs and have a common paying account. Also, we will create one VPC with four subnets across two AZs per BU.

In order to design for the VPC, we need to assign the IP address blocks. There are a variety of ways we can do that, however, there is normally a simple formula that I use. We will use a RFC 1918 address (private IP address), which is basically `10.x.x.x`, `172.16.x.x` – `172.31.x.x`, `192.168.x.x`.

We can create the IP address:

- **First octet**: Location/type of infrastructure
- **Second octet**: Business unit
- **Third octet**: Subnet function
- **Fourth octet**: Host IP address

Now remember, any schema can work, however ensure you have a schema for the IP addressing so you don't have any discontiguous networks, and it assists in the logical routing.

In our schema, we can have all data centers/privates starting with `172.16-31.x.x`, the public cloud would be `10.x.x.x`, and a CoLo could be `192.168.x.x`.

The second unit can be business unit/region combination - for example, we can simply say the first digit of the second octet being 1, could mean the Americas, 2 could be Asia, and so on. This can work with 10.x, but not for any other subnet.

The third octet can be a subnet function—such as production web, production DB, non-prod web, and so on.

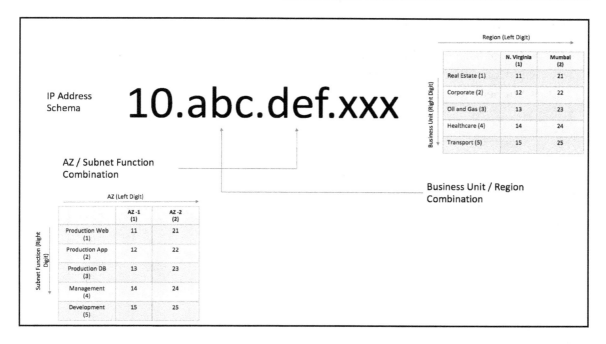

I hope the preceding image explains the schema that is used for subnetting (feel free to use any schema that works for you). The following table is the output of the schema for a particular BU.

Remember this needs to be implemented for every VPC that is created:

Region	VPC Subnet	Subnet function	Subnets
N. Virginia	10.11.x.x/16	Production Web (AZ-1)	10.11.11.x /24
		Production App (AZ-1)	10.11.12.x/24
		Production DB (AZ-1)	10.11.13.x/24
		Production Web (AZ-2)	10.11.21.x/24
		Production App (AZ-2)	10.11.22.x/24
		Production DB (AZ-3)	10.11.23.x/24
Mumbai	10.21.x.x/16	Production Web (AZ-1)	10.21.11.x/24
		Production App (Az-1)	10.21.12.x/24

With this in mind, let's look at the design:

- No. of accounts: six (five for the BU's, and one paying)
- No. of VPCs: one VPC per region
- Subnets: four subnets per VPC (two per AZ)

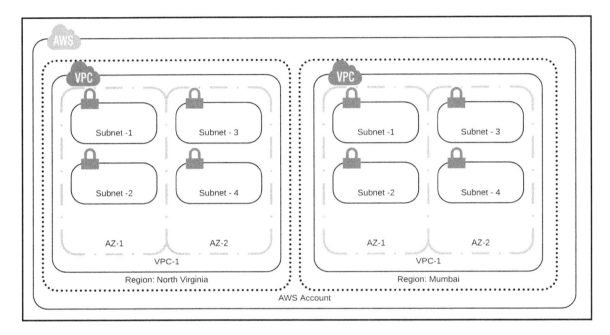

There is nothing stopping us from designing each VPC different to the others. The design of a single account would look something like this. The preceding diagram should also help clarify the hierarchy and the concepts.

In the preceding diagram, we see that the particular BU has two VPCs, one in Mumbai, the other in North Virginia and each of them have a single VPC. In this book, we will not be using the full fledged example, but will simply be using a single VPC in a single region to show the configurations. These can later be extrapolated to any design.

Connectivity to the private cloud

Now, since we have designed the VPCs themselves, it's time for connectivity. From previous chapters, you know that we can do this using a VPN or direct connect. In this case, since there is not going to be much traffic, we will simply create a VPN connecting to our VPC.

There is something that we must keep in mind while designing multiple VPCs. We have the ability to use transit VPCs. This simply means that we can connect from our data center to the transit VPC, and then connect the transit VPC to the other VPCs. While this keeps the routing simple, remember that if the VPCs are in different regions, data transfer charges apply. Refer the following links for more information:

- http://docs.aws.amazon.com/solutions/latest/cisco-based-transit-vpc/welcome.html
- https://aws.amazon.com/blogs/aws/aws-solution-transit-vpc/

The following diagram will show the connectivity options from a single VPC:

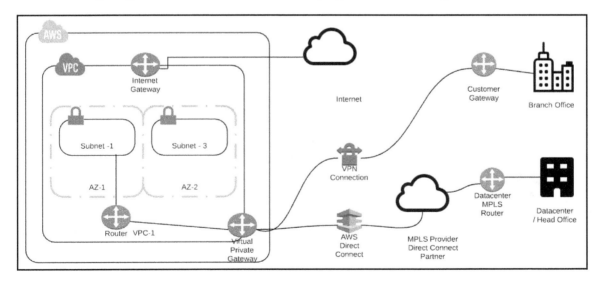

We remember from the previous section, that a **Subnet** is a zonal service and is created in an AZ. So, the AWS structure shown previously will be familiar to you from the previous section, however some other points to understand in the previous diagram are:

- Each VPC has an implied router (**Router**)
- The routing table is associated per subnet (**Subnet-1** and **Subnet-3**)
- The **Virtual Private Gateway** (**VGW**) is the AWS side of a direct connect or VPN connection (connection going back in-house)
- The **Internet Gateway** (**IGW**) is the AWS side of the internet connection associated with the VPC

Remember, in the previous section of the book, we mentioned *public* and *private* AWS subnets. A subnet whose routing table doesn't have an entry for the Internet Gateway is considered a private subnet.

Also, in order to see all of it at work, another few basic concepts about networking that we should remember are as follows:

- A network device needs only determine the next hop and not the full path:
    - Switches use a MAC address table to determine where they have to put the packet next.
    - Routers use one or more routing protocols to determine the next hop. It might use some protocols such as OSPF (running on a Dijkstra algorithm) in order to know all the available paths to determine the next hop, but ultimately, it's simply the **next hop**.
- A network device consults its local table in order to determine this next hop.
- A network device *normally* finds its next hop based on the *destination* address and *not* the source address (please remember that this is source-based routing, which is an advanced networking concept and doesn't fall under the purview of this book).
- The most specific match is always used, which means the more specific the route, the more preferred it is:
    - The order of priority is - find the most specific route, if multiple routes are found with the same specificity, then use the route learnt from the better routing protocol. Then, once all computation is done, just find the next hop.

With this in mind, we can see in the following diagram, how the routing table of the subnet combined with the routing table of the IGW and VGW help in sending packets to the right places:

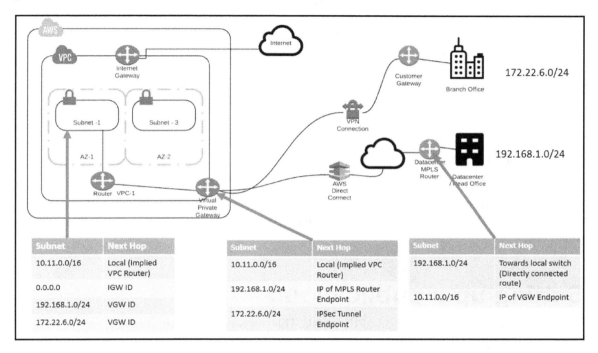

Subnet	Next Hop		Subnet	Next Hop		Subnet	Next Hop
10.11.0.0/16	Local (Implied VPC Router)		10.11.0.0/16	Local (Implied VPC Router)		192.168.1.0/24	Towards local switch (Directly connected route)
0.0.0.0	IGW ID		192.168.1.0/24	IP of MPLS Router Endpoint		10.11.0.0/16	IP of VGW Endpoint
192.168.1.0/24	VGW ID		172.22.6.0/24	IPSec Tunnel Endpoint			
172.22.6.0/24	VGW ID						

We know that our VPC has the subnet `10.11.0.0/16` created. The subnet routing table tells the packet to go to the implied router if it is for the VPC, or send it for the VGW if it is for two of the subnets (our subnets back in the remote office and head office). For everything else, please send it to the Internet Gateway (IGW).

The subnet's routing table doesn't know or care how the VGW will send the packet - direct connect or the IPSec tunnel. That is because of the previously mentioned basic principles; it only needs to know the next HOP.

Also notice that the same routing table has the route for both the IGW and VGW, so how does it know which to use? Again, we see specific routes pointed to VGW and the default route to the IGW. This again is the principle of *specific routing is preferred*, so if a packet comes for destination `4.2.2.2`, then it will see that the specific routes don't match, and hence will send it to the IGW.

Also, take a look at the routing table of the MPLS router on the customer's end. It has a route pointing in the opposite direction, because the return packet will have the same destination as our VPC.

> The direct connect and the VPN can both be terminated on the same device at the customer's end. This is normally done if we want the VPN to be the backup of the direct connection.
>
> It could even be set up with load balancing, with high priority traffic going through the direct connection and low priority through VPN. You might want to consider this if bandwidth on the MPLS is expensive or low when compared to the internet.

Having understood the design principles and the connectivity in the AWS, let's set a VPC ourselves, which we will use for our hybrid cloud exercises in the book.

We will be creating a single account, in which a single VPC will be created in a single region. We will then be creating a Virtual Gateway and creating a VPN connection to our data center.

Setting up a public cloud – AWS

We are finally at the *doing* section of the book. The steps we will follow to accomplish the aforementioned tasks are:

- Create an account in AWS
- Create a VPC
- Create and configure a VGW
- Create subnets and view the routing table

Once we are done, we will set up an access and secret key in order to be able to use the API calls to AWS.

Creating an account in AWS

For the purposes of the book, we can create an account in AWS. If you have an existing account, we can use that too.

We can create an AWS account by visiting `https://aws.amazon.com/free/` and click on **Create a Free Account**:

1. You will be taken to **Create a New AWS Account**, fill in the preliminary details, you will be taken to a new screen.
2. Choose **Company Account** or **Personal Account**. (Choose personal—if you are using it for personal testing or following along).
3. Type the requested account information, and then choose Create account.
4. Enter **Payment/Card details**—do not worry, if you stick to using free tier services, you will not be charged.

It will then verify you and ask for the support services. Please choose basic (included) if you are simply following along.

 Depending on the region and country you select, you may be asked some questions. For example for India, you might be asked PAN number, and so on. However, the wizard is intuitive, and you should have no difficulty in following it.

Once the account is created, you can click on take me to the management console:

The screens may vary, but in essence we should be able to log into the console. At first glance, the console looks daunting, but navigating will be easy once you familiarize yourself with the services (links to which were given earlier in the chapter).

If you have created a new personal account, you may have to click on **Login with root credentials** to access your console.

The whole list of services and their functionality will require a book on its own, so instead of digressing, I encourage you guys to explore them on your own before continuing.

Creating a VPC and subnets

If you guys have created the account, please remember that a VPC would have been created by default (in every region) and we can use that. However, in order to understand the concepts, we will create a new one.

From the top of the Console, Click on **Services**, and then find **VPC** (by scrolling or typing it in the search box):

Also, in the top-right corner, choose the region where you want the VPC. (Please remember that the VPC is a regional service):

1. Click on **Create VPC**.
2. Fill in the **VPC CIDR** (this will be the supernet, from which all the subnets can be created).
3. Choose **Tenancy**:
    - If you need HIPAA compliance, you need to select **Dedicated tenancy** - this means your hypervisor will not be shared with any other tenants, but you will be charged more.

4. Click on **Create**:

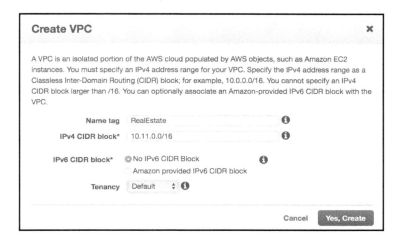

This will create the VPC. Please remember, by default, there will be the default VPCs and the subnets associated with it. You can create a new subnet for this VPC.

Click on **Subnets** on the left, click on **Add**, select your VPC, and add the subnet. We will add the Production Web Subnet. We could choose the **Availability Zone** or let the system choose it for us:

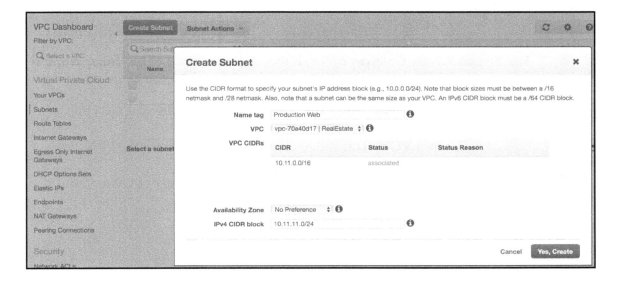

The next step, is to create the Internet Gateways, the Virtual Private Gateways, and VPN connections.

Creating the IGW and VGW

There is a default Internet Gateway for the VPC, however, creating another is simple, as it only needs a name and can then be used in the routing table. The following steps needs to be perform for creating the IGW and VGW:

1. On the left-hand side, click on **Internet Gateways** and click on **Create**. All we have to do is give it a name (which is also optional) and a default gateway forwarder will be created:

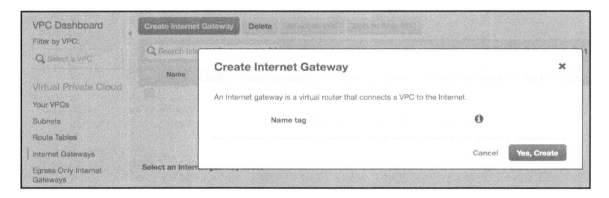

2. The **Virtual Private Gateway** option is found under **VPN Connections**. In order to configure a VPN connection, there are, essentially, three things we must do on the AWS side:
   - **Define the customer gateway**: This is the IP address of the VPN hardware/software device on the enterprise side
   - **Create a VGW**: This is the router on the AWS side of the VPN connection
   - **VPN routing options**: We can have static routing or BGP routing

3. Creation of the VGW is straightforward. Give it a name and we are done:

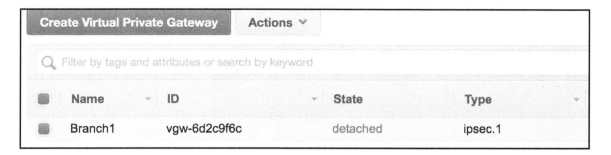

4. The Customer Gateway needs two values, a name and IP. It also asks if we want to statically route it, or enable BGP routing:

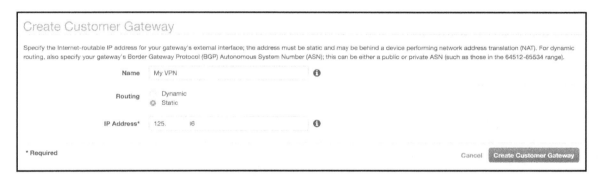

5. The final step is to create the VPN connection. On the left pane, click on **VPN Connection**, associate the **Virtual Private Gateway** and **Customer Gateway** that you created, and click on **Create VPN**:

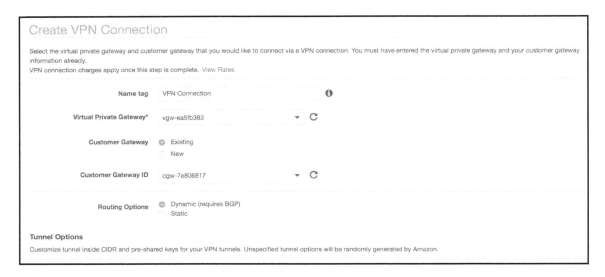

6. Once the VPN Connection is created, you can download the configuration for the peer device by clicking on **Download Configuration** in various formats:

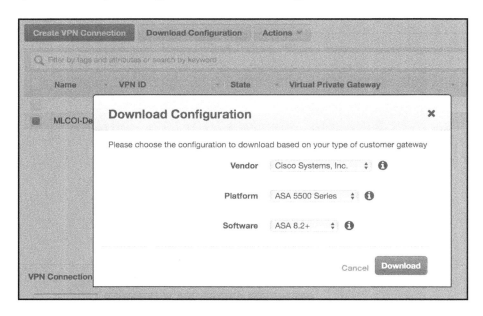

Once you have downloaded the configuration and set it up on the other end, the VPN tunnel will go active.

 Visit `http://docs.aws.amazon.com/AmazonVPC/latest/UserGuide/VPC_ VPN.html` for the different configuration options of the VPN.

Setting up AWS API access

When setting up an account, we can choose to provide an access key and secret key to the user that they can then use to make API calls to the AWS cloud. We will need AWS API keys to use an Orchestrator in the next chapter.

The access to AWS is controlled via IAM. So, in order to create a user with API access, we will choose IAM from the list of services:

1. On the left pane, choose **Users**.
2. Click on **Add User**.
3. Set the **User Name**, **Password**.
4. Choose **Programmatic access** in the access type (in addition, you could choose Console access also).
5. Click on **Next:**.

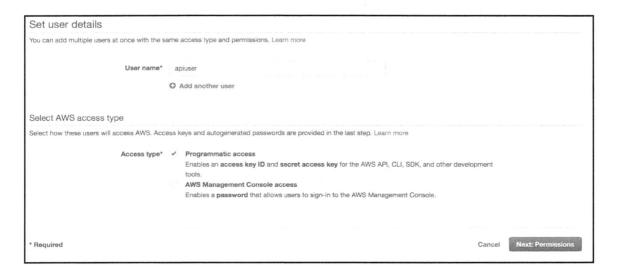

6. In the next section, you will set permissions. While IAM has a finely grained role, for the purposes of the exercise, we will set it to administrative user and click on **Next**, where you will review the user:

Once created, you will see the access key and secret key. You need to keep them safe.

Don't put the secret key in bespoke code of an application that you intend to share, even for compiled code, as it can be easily decompiled. If the API calls that you will be making are going to be run from EC2 instances, please use IAM Roles, rather than using an access key and secret key.

	User	Access key ID		Secret access key
▶ ⊘	apiuser	AKIA	37Q	********* Show

Once we have the API keys, we can use a whole host of scripting/programming languages to make HTTP RESTful calls. The access and secret key are akin to user credentials for authenticating the API calls being made.

As a sample, the following Python code fetches the list of virtual machines, we will first store the AWS credentials in a file at the location ~/.aws/credentials . The content of the file will be the access and secret key

```
[default]
aws_access_key_id=<Insert Access Key here>
aws_secret_access_key=<Insert Secret Key here>
```

Once the file has been created, we can then

```
import boto
from boto import ec2
ec2 = boto.ec2.connect_to_region('us-west-2', profile_name='default')
response = ec2.get_all_instances()
instances = [i for r in reservations for i in r.instances]
for i in instances:
    print (i)
```

The hyper clouds have their **Software Development Kit** (**SDK**) for most major platforms, such as .NET, Python, Java, Go, and so on. Under normal circumstances, the API access and secret key is used, where the software is on-premises and is trying to talk to AWS endpoints.

So, for example, you have an application on AWS, whose app server is trying to push/pull some files from S3. You shouldn't use the access and secret key (you could, but there are alternatives), you should use the IAM roles.

So the bottom line, as a rule of thumb, is that the access key and secret key should be a part of configuration and not code, and should be protected like a username and password would be.

Setting up the private cloud

If we wanted to take a pragmatic approach, the public cloud that is now connected to our data center could also become a simplistic hybrid cloud, but we will set up a private OpenStack cloud to take it a notch higher.

In the last chapter, we learnt about the architecture of OpenStack. There are a variety of ways to set up OpenStack. We can use several install methods such as Juju Charms, OpenStack Ansible (OSA), and so on. But for our example, we will install a DevStack OpenStack instance on a single server.

The DevStack install is *not* a production-ready deployment, it is used for development. However, for the purposes of explaining the private cloud, this will be more than sufficient. We will look at some of the design principles for it before we go to the actual implementation.

The installation of production-grade OpenStack systems is beyond the purview of this book. Refer the OpenStack documentation that can be found at: `https://docs.openstack.org/install-guide/`. There are other books that cover these topics, so please refer to them for more details.

Basics of designing an OpenStack environment

Truth be told, DevStack can be installed with a **single** command for most instances of DevStack that are normally run on developers' machines, so there is no need to design it. However, when deploying OpenStack to a production environment, one definitely needs to take a look at the design of it.

OpenStack, since its inception in 2010, has moved on from being a simple cloud orchestration layer to a full-fledged cloud operating system. This is the only one on the market with such abilities, and the support from the community has become quite an untameable system, which quickly becomes a double-edged sword depending on how it is designed and deployed.

If we design it right, we have a powerful hyper-scale ready, multi-featured, multi-tenanted, service down cloud, otherwise, we have an unmanageable mess on our hands. Therefore, we need to take care when broaching the topic of OpenStack design.

In this section, the idea is to design an OpenStack environment using a fictitious use case, from our favorite Acme Inc.. This will show our thought process when designing the OpenStack environment. So the use case is as follows:

> *"Our competitors have started gaining on us in terms of agility due to the introduction of the cloud. We need to also make our development teams agile, by providing them with self-service and programmable infrastructure. However, since we have heavily invested in upgrading the in-house infrastructure, and for compliance reasons, we will prefer that this cloud be in- house".*
>
> *- Acme Inc.*

Now, we can deduce a few things:

- It needs to be private cloud - as the company has already invested in in-house infrastructure
- It needs to be a service down cloud - as we need a programmable infrastructure, or Infrastructure as Code
- The use case will be *development* and *testing*

Now, from our first few chapters, I am sure you realize that the best solution to this problem statement will be OpenStack. If it was both a public and private use case, we could have used Azure Stack as well.

Since we have made the choice to go with OpenStack, in order to further design it, we will ask the following questions in order to determine the capability of the cloud, usage, and so on:

Area	Questions	Decision points impacted
Capability	The development team needs DBaaS	Install the OpenStack project `Trove`
	The development team needs Container as a Service	Install the OpenStack project `Magnum`
	The development team uses big data / Hadoop clusters and needs that as a service	Install the OpenStack project `Sahara`
	You intend to offer a Dropbox kind of service inhouse	Install the OpenStack project `Swift`
	The developers need to be able to spin up bare-metal servers	Install the OpenStack project `Ironic`
	You would need the system to be able to measure and charge back	Install the OpenStack project `Ceilometer` and `Cloud Kitty`
	Do you need CPU pinning/NUMA on your host?	Designing the OpenStack Project *Nova*
	Are there different kinds of hardware that we want to use with OpenStack?	Designing the host clusters and availability zones in Nova
Scale	How many data centers will OpenStack be working with?	Helps design the Keystone and Horizon appropriately
	How many physical hypervisors will be used in total?	Helps design Nova cells and so on
Support	Do we need 99.99% uptime for OpenStack itself?	Helps design the data path and control components
	Do we need external vendor support?	Helps choose which OpenStack distribution to use
	What hypervisor support do we need?	Helps choose which OpenStack distribution to use

This is the mere tip of the iceberg, but you get the idea. First-level questions help choose which OpenStack projects need to be installed and the support questions would help us choose which distribution of OpenStack to use.

There will then be second-level questions based on how each of the services are configured, and they could fill a book of their own. However for this exercise, we will simply choose a distribution and deployment method.

Choosing an OpenStack distribution

An OpenStack distribution is chosen based on the following things:

- Vendor support
- Hypervisor support
- Familiarity with the underlying OS
- Ease of management
- Ease of upgrades

Please remember that most companies that have an OpenStack distribution have paid enterprise support for them. Community support is also very good, albeit not SLA-driven. There are also specialist companies that only perform OpenStack support—for example, Mirantis. There are also some companies that provide an OpenStack hosted private cloud—for example Platform9. They provide the control layer of OpenStack in the cloud, but the data path is in your data center.

That being said, vendor support is not relevant to this section. Upgrades are seamless in automated deployments, so they also become slightly irrelevant here, but may be relevant in the next section. Hence, the choice is between Hypervisor support, OS support, and the familiarity of the OpenStack OS.

Note that the table doesn't take into account the Ocata and later releases of OpenStack:

Distribution name	Hypervisor support	OS support
Ubuntu OpenStack	Hyper-V, QEMU, KVM, ESXi, LXC, LxD	Linux, Windows
Red Hat OpenStack	ESXi, KVM	Linux, Windows
VMWare Integrated OpenStack	ESXi	Linux, Windows

Mirantis OpenStack	Xen, Docker, Hyper-V, ESXi, LXC, QEMU, KVM	Linux, Windows
Oracle OpenStack for Solaris	Solaris	Solaris
Oracle OpenStack	Xen, KVM	Linux, Windows, Solaris
Cisco OpenStack	QEMU, KVM	Linux, Windows
IBM Cloud Manager	z/VM, PowerVM, ESXi, Hyper-V, KVM	Linux, Windows
Suse Cloud	Xen, Hyper-V, ESXi, KVM	Linux, Windows
Dell Red Hat Cloud	KVM	Linux, Windows
HP Helion OpenStack	ESXi, KVM	Linux, Windows

Choosing the deployment method

Once the distribution is chosen, we move on to the deployment method. The most popular, automated deployment methods are as follows:

- Red Hat OpenStack: RDO Deployment, OSA (OpenStack Ansible)
- Ubuntu: MaaS (Metal as a Service) and Juju
- VIO: VMware vSphere
- Mirantis OpenStack: Fuel

We can also build the OpenStack environment manually. However, in the future, more and more people will be putting their *control layer* of OpenStack into containers, and for that you may be able to use Kolla or Stackanetes.

For a production OpenStack environment, we now need to design the following:

- Network
- Storage
- Compute
- Configuration

Installing DevStack

Since we have had a brief brush with how to design an OpenStack environment, let's install DevStack. The DevStack script (for lack of a better word) was intended for developers to create a personal OpenStack environment with the projects that they needed. While DevStack can have a multiple node installations (distributed), we will simply concentrate on a single node.

It has a single configuration file, which can be modified in order to tell it which projects to install and the configurations of them. All you need is a single Linux server that is supported - RHEL and Ubuntu. Please remember, all the projects that are going to be installed on the same server so we will need a beefier machine.

Our Linux server has the following:

- OS: Ubuntu 16.04 LTS
- RAM: 16 GB
- CPU: 4
- Hard disk: 100 GB

Please remember, even if you have a smaller machine, it will still work. You could even run DevStack on a virtual machine, as a matter of fact, I will be using a virtual machine to deploy DevStack.

Log in to the server and clone the DevStack repository.

Once your server is ready, log in to it using SSH and then clone the DevStack. We are using `git` to clone the Ocata branch of OpenStack code. If you don't specify the branch, the latest commit will be used:

```
cd /
sudo git clone https://git.openstack.org/openstack-dev/devstack -b
stable/ocata
```

Once the cloning is complete, a directory called `devstack` will be created:

```
alokshrivastwa@instance-1:/$ cd /
alokshrivastwa@instance-1:/$ sudo git clone https://git.openstack.org/openstack-dev/devstack -b stable/ocata
Cloning into 'devstack'...
remote: Counting objects: 40365, done.
remote: Compressing objects: 100% (19957/19957), done.
remote: Total 40365 (delta 28692), reused 30997 (delta 19787)
Receiving objects: 100% (40365/40365), 8.16 MiB | 13.45 MiB/s, done.
Resolving deltas: 100% (28692/28692), done.
Checking connectivity... done.
```

We can change to the devstack directory and copy the configuration file (local.conf) into the main folder:

```
cd devstack/
sudo cp samples/local.conf local.conf
```

The local.conf file determines the projects that will be installed and also the other configuration options.

Configuring DevStack to enable Heat

Let's take a look at the default local.conf file that is copied from the samples. In the following snippet, I have removed the comments, however, please look at the full file as the comments show several different configuration options:

```
alokshrivastwa@instance-1:/devstack$ cat local.conf | grep -v "#" | grep -v
"^$"
[[local|localrc]]
ADMIN_PASSWORD=nomoresecret
DATABASE_PASSWORD=stackdb
RABBIT_PASSWORD=stackqueue
SERVICE_PASSWORD=$ADMIN_PASSWORD
LOGFILE=$DEST/logs/stack.sh.log
LOGDAYS=2
SWIFT_HASH=66a3d6b56c1f479c8b4e70ab5c2000f5
SWIFT_REPLICAS=1
SWIFT_DATA_DIR=$DEST/data
```

We can see that we can set the database password, the AMQP (RabbitMQ) password, and so on. In this file, we will install the Heat project.

In the ENABLED_SERVICES, we will append all the Heat services for the project to be installed.

If you are wondering what Heat is, Heat is an Infrastructure as Code component of OpenStack. It is equivalent to CloudFormation in AWS, and ARM (Azure Resource Manager) templates in Azure.

We are installing Heat because the IaaC is a unique feature of a service down cloud, and we want our private cloud to be service down. We can also use the Heat templates to create a full blown application in later chapters.

We will edit the `local.conf` file to look as follows (we have simply enabled Heat services and changed passwords):

```
alokshrivastwa@instance-1:/devstack$ cat local.conf | grep -v "#" | grep -v "^$"
[[local|localrc]]
ADMIN_PASSWORD=pass4adminUser
DATABASE_PASSWORD=stackdb
RABBIT_PASSWORD=stackqueue
SERVICE_PASSWORD=pass4OpenStackServices
ENABLED_SERVICES+=,heat,h-api,h-api-cfn,h-api-cw,h-eng

LOGFILE=$DEST/logs/stack.sh.log
LOGDAYS=2
SWIFT_HASH=66a3d6b56c1f479c8b4e70ab5c2000f5
SWIFT_REPLICAS=1
SWIFT_DATA_DIR=$DEST/data
alokshrivastwa@instance-1:/devstack$
```

Once it is done, it's simply a matter of creating a user and running the `devstack` script:

```
sudo /devstack/tools/create-stack-user.sh
>sudo chown -R stack:stack /devstack
sudo su stack
/devstack/stack.sh
```

The preceding commands invoke the script to create a user called `stack`, changes the ownership of the `devstack` folder to it, and finally changes to the stack user and executes the command `stack.sh` to install the Devstack.

Now, sit back and relax. Depending on your internet connection speed, your DevStack will be ready to go.

It is highly recommended that you use a `screen` command in Linux, so that even if you get disconnected from the SSH terminal during the DevStack install, the install will not fail. Otherwise, the long running script will stop if the SSH gets disconnected.

The `devstack` runs the individual OpenStack services in screens of their own, so in order to debug, you have to go to the appropriate screen.

Once your OpenStack installation is completed (using DevStack), you will be presented with a screen displaying the information to log in to the OpenStack environment:

```
===========================
DevStack Component Timing
===========================
Total runtime           661

run_process              55
test_with_retry           3
apt-get-update            2
pip_install              78
restart_apache_server    14
wait_for_service         15
apt-get                  11
===========================



This is your host IP address: 10.128.0.2
This is your host IPv6 address: ::1
Horizon is now available at http://10.128.0.2/dashboard
Keystone is serving at http://10.128.0.2/identity/
The default users are: admin and demo
The password: pass4adminUser
DevStack Version: ocata
```

You can now log in to the IP address using the username `admin` and the password that we set.

> Since, this is a DevStack install, it will not survive a reboot. Remember to execute `/devstack/unstack.sh` and `/devstack/stack.sh` in order to re-initialize. Also note that any configuration that you have done in DevStack will get overwritten.

Summary

In this chapter, we have seen the architectural patterns of how AWS and OpenStack is architected, and we have established a VPN connection between the AWS environment and our data center. We will start using this system in the following chapters.

6
Building a Traditional CMP-Based Hybrid Cloud

In the previous chapters, we learned the different meanings that one could attach to the hybrid cloud, and also the different use cases and designs that can be done for each of them. Now, having followed the last chapter, we should have a VPC created in AWS and also our DevStack ready and raring to go.

In this chapter, we will see how we can build a hybrid cloud that is created for the *Supporting Applications Use Case* and also the *Isolated/Distributed Use Case* (as discussed in `Chapter 2`, *Hybrid Cloud – Why Does It Matter?*) with the help of a Cloud Management Platform (CMP).

The CMP that we will be using here is ManageIQ, however, we could use other orchestrators in the market ranging from COTS products such as VMware's vRealize Suite, Right Scale CMP, and so on, to FOSS products such as OneOps (`http://oneops.com`) and even OpenNebula (but OpenNebula is more of an OpenStack replacement rather than an orchestrator).

Supporting applications use case

If you are interested in this topic, you are most likely looking to fix the limitations, or enhance the capabilities, of what I call *Invisible Applications*. These are applications most people in an organization sometimes won't even know about the existence of until a disaster strikes, and at other times would be taken for granted.

I am talking about the following, well-known services:

- Backup and disaster recovery
- File sharing

As you can see, these are mainly storage related services, and so before we go on to see how the capability of these can be augmented and enhanced using the public cloud, let's take a look at the traditional way of performing these actions.

Traditional operations

Traditionally, there were three kinds of networked/centralized storage systems in an enterprise in addition to the directly attached storage that may have come with the servers:

- **Storage Area Network (SAN)** - block level storage
- **Network Attached Storage (NAS)** - file level storage (a.k.a Binary Large Object Storage)
- Tape storage - archive storage

Block storage is something that you can attach to a machine and then format and put a filesystem on, so a SAN can be considered akin to a local disk connected with a long network cable.

BLOB storage/file storage is a system where you can store files without bothering about the filesystem, block size, and so on.

While there are other differences between NAS and SAN (NAS is normally a single device and SAN is a network that connects multiple storage devices), they have seen a convergence in recent times as SAN storage controllers have gained functionality.

Due to this convergence, the kind of storage that is being used, unlike the past, is no longer dependent on the hardware that is serving it, but dependent on the protocol that is being used to fetch it.

If you are using SCSI - it doesn't matter if you use it on a SATA/PATA (IDE) cable for directly attached storage, SCSI on a fiber channel/fiber channel over Ethernet, or iSCSI (Internet SCSI) running on any TCP/IP stack, we are using block storage.

On the other hand, if we are using protocols such as NFS, SMB, or CIFS, then we are using object storage or file storage.

Having understood the basics, let's take a look at how the services that we are interested in have been consumed traditionally.

As storage became the key system and possibly the most precious system (*your data stays here*), the industry started moving away from individual disks (such as those connected in your personal computers), to a more centralized storage, in the form of NAS and SAN.

Centralized storage appliances obviously had disk arrays, and in order to protect data loss due to failure of a single disk, several **Redundant Array of Independent Disks (RAID)** systems were created.

These centralized storage systems came with their own controllers (sometimes two of them for redundancy) and they were responsible for ensuring data integrity and accessibility over various protocols. These controllers served the data on SCSI over FC and sometimes iSCSI.

These centralized systems (both NAS and SAN) were typically backed up to a tape drive and in many cases, the tapes were dispatched physically to another secure location for storage.

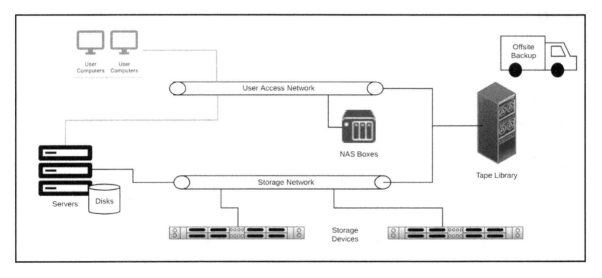

The preceding diagram shows the whole process. As you can see, there were two different networks (the user and the storage networks). Originally, the **Storage network** used the relatively expensive fiber for its physical layer, and fiber channel as the layer 2 protocol in order to serve up the SCSI.

The **user network** had a physical copper (CAT-5/5e/6) network running Ethernet as its layer 2 protocol and TCP/IP on top of it. The user network was relatively slower and inexpensive.

NAS boxes are traditionally just another endpoint on the user network, and they were used to store the user files. The storage devices exposed LUNs on RAID disks, and were mounted as disks on the servers.

The tape storage was connected to either the user network, storage network, or even both, they wrote the data serially on a magnetic tape, were used to archive the data, and were the primary backup system of the company. DR was taken care of by physically moving the tapes to another location and then restoring it at that location.

Modern outlook

As the technology grew, we started collapsing the user and storage networks. This is done by using protocols such as FCoE and iSCSI. We also started collapsing the NAS and SAN, by ensuring the SAN controllers also have the ability to serve the NAS protocols.

The SAN controllers also started managing multiple types of disk and intelligently saving/accessing data on various storage depending upon the access frequency of that data. This is called storage tiering.

As we moved to software defined storage, the storage appliances also started allowing IOPS control programmatically and this, in addition to the storage tiering, made the storage system be defined programmatically.

So, now one could create a LUN and set the policies on it programmatically. The controllers also allow for having the public cloud as one of its storage tiers. The following diagram shows the operation of the storage tiering and the convergence:

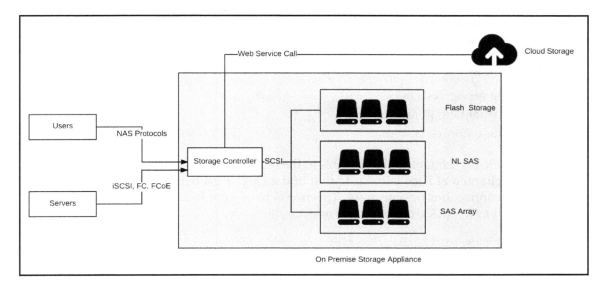

As shown in the diagram, the storage controller can save the infrequent or archived data directly in the cloud, so the backup and DR becomes easy.

Now, let us consider the benefits of having a storage tier as the cloud or even the archival in the cloud. Backing up and archiving to the cloud saves the cost of shipping the tapes and the time it takes to do so. Also, the cloud is elastic, virtually infinite, and pay per use, so we will save on capacity management.

It seems like a no-brainer; this is immensely helpful. Now let's ask ourselves, *"do we really need to use modern and expensive storage boxes with high end storage controllers in order to do this?"* This will lead to the question of whether it is easy to implement.

The answer to the preceding question is *"No"*. There are several services in the public cloud that provide free backup and DR. For storage tiering, we could even use the OpenSDS project (https://www.opensds.io) on top of existing SAN products to provide the required features.

Using the AWS storage gateway

Now, that we know about the traditional and modern outlook of the storage, let's now start with the storage gateway service of AWS, which allows us to use its Cloud as a tier. This is known as *hybrid cloud storage*.

In addition to allowing us to do backups to the cloud, we can also use the system to run a few batch processes, or burst any application that doesn't need real-time data in the cloud.

The AWS hybrid gateway can be used as:

- A file server system
- A virtual tape library
- A block storage system

Please remember that *uploads* to the cloud are free, but downloads are charged at a fee (similar to that of data leaving a region) on VPN connections or otherwise. This needs to be kept in mind before connecting it as a block storage device or even file server.

Please read https://aws.amazon.com/storagegateway/ for more use cases and examples. Please see http://aws.amazon.com/storagegateway/pricing for pricing.

First order of business is to choose the region of the storage gateway. Remember, at the time of writing the storage gateway was only present in 14 regions. More regions may be supported. You need to visit http://docs.aws.amazon.com/storagegateway/latest/userguide/available-regions-intro.html to select the region.

Once you have selected the region, the major steps are as follows:

- Creating a storage gateway device configuration on AWS
- Creating the storage gateway on-premises
- Opening network ports

For the full configuration process, refer to: http://docs.aws.amazon.com/storagegateway/latest/userguide/create-gateway-file.html.

Now let's take a look at the way the storage gateway systems would work. Things to keep in mind are as follows:

- The devices (storage gateway) will be present locally in the data center
- They will have local storage
- They will have an internet connection and will be connected to the public cloud

With this is mind, let's check the architecture of the different gateways.

File gateway

This is the simplest type of deployment, where the backend is the S3 Storage. It exposes the NFS protocol to the clients. The disk that is connected to the storage gateway is used to hold the data for the amount of time the data is not stored in the backend and for the frequently accessed data.

The backend connection could be on VPN, Direct Connect or even the internet. Since the S3 endpoint is SSL encrypted, the data encryption in motion is taken care of. The S3 buckets can be encrypted on the server side, thereby securing the data at rest. We could allow Amazon to manage the keys using S3 or the Key Management System (KMS).

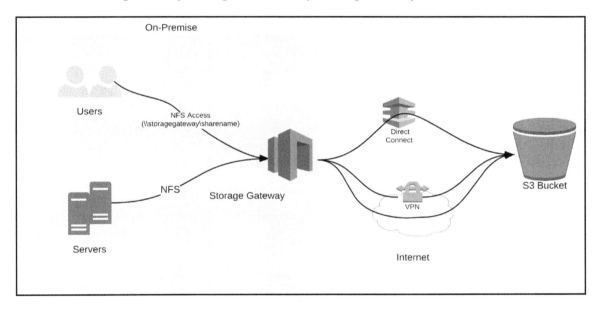

Running the SSL within the IPSec VPN simply provides an additional layer of transport security, but does make the transmission a little slower. However, this can be considered if there is already an existing VPN connection to the VPC from the enterprise.

Volume gateways

The second function that the storage gateway functions with is the volume gateway. In this we also have two types:

- Cached volume gateways
- Stored volume gateways

The primary difference between the two is, in the cached mode, the disks are completely written in S3 and only the cache is maintained locally. However in stored volume gateways, the amount of disk that is given to the storage gateway appliance is your maximum storage that can be exposed, as that is the primary storage, and S3 simply creates a volume snapshot.

The cached volume gateway is technically used to architect the solution of having a large, but a relatively slow (Random Reads) storage solution, as this depends on the internet / direct connect speed exposed to the on-premises system, with the ability to move those servers to the cloud when needed.

The stored volume gateways on the other hand are a good option for comparatively faster storage (Random Reads), as it has local storage but invoking the DR is simpler, as all the disks would have snapshots (EBS Snapshots) on AWS for us to use.

The following diagram shows the operations of both kinds of volume gateway:

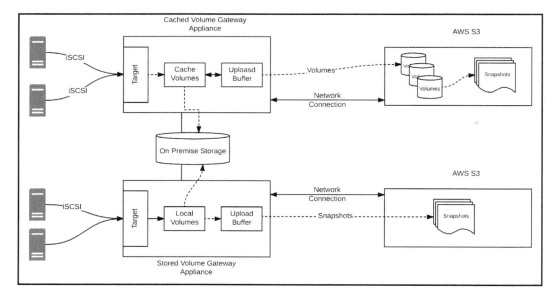

From an architect's point of view, refer to the following table in order to understand the reasons one may choose one over the other:

Requirement	Cached volume gateway	Stored volume gateway
Size of storage to be exposed to the servers needs to be more than the storage attached to the appliance	**Yes** - This system caches the frequently accessed storage and allows volumes from 1 GB to 32 TB from S3. The size of the cache is dependent on the storage attached to the appliance	**No** - The gateway uses the cloud only to create snapshots, and the storage exposed cannot exceed the storage connected to the appliance
Disaster recovery	**Yes** - Volumes can be created out of the snapshot	**Yes** - Volumes can be created out of the snapshot
Virtual machine migration	**Yes** - EBS Volumes can be created out of snapshots and attached to EC2 instances	**Yes** - EBS Volumes can be created out of snapshots and attached to EC2 instances
Lower random read time	No - The system caches the frequently accessed data, however, in the random read if an infrequent data is requested, it will need to be fetched from S3 over the network	**Yes** - Since all the data is locally available, the random read doesn't need to access S3 over the network

I hope this also clarifies the usage and the architecture decisions made while choosing the system.

Tape gateway

The final mode of deployment is to deploy the storage gateway appliance in tape library mode. As the name implies, it exposes itself as a tape drive would, which means you can connect it to your existing backup application with the same protocol.

One the backend, it saves the tape backups on S3. Once you move them to an archive, on the backend, it uses Amazon Glacier in order to archive the data.

At the time of writing, a tape library using the tape gateway can store up to 1500 tapes or 1 PB of data.

If you are wondering where you would use this, it is often used when you need to replace an existing robotic tape library and also offsite backup/archival process.

Isolated/distributed application use case

This is the second most requested feature by enterprises. A *single pane of glass* for provisioning the resources in the cloud. This led to the creation of Cloud Management Platforms.

While they are called *management platforms*, one of the most important features they provide is provisioning. The life cycle services they support start with provisioning. CMPs also provide an API of their own, which allows the enterprises to communicate with the CMPs programmatically, thereby integrating it with other enterprise applications:

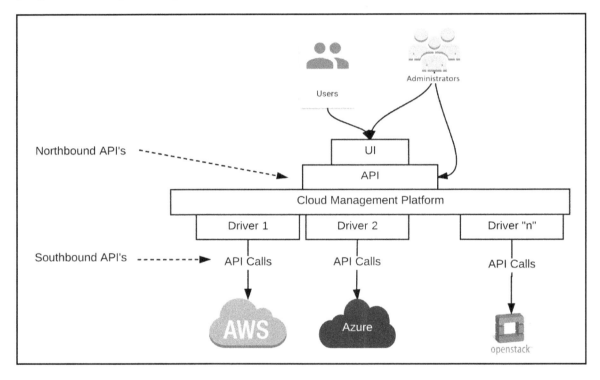

The APIs that are used to connect to the CMP itself are normally called **Northbound APIs** and the API calls being made to the various cloud platforms are dubbed **Southbound APIs**.

The APIs could be of many types, but mainly, RESTful APIs are used in the cloud. There are several CMPs on the market as we have discussed, each of them have a specialization and a reason to exist. It's a good idea to compare these when choosing the right one.

Remember that for the most part, CMPs work mainly with a virtual machine and not PaaS services. However, some CMPs allow for extensibility and integration.

Let's take a look at the following table of four **Cloud Management Platforms** with various aspects. This is simply to show the process that one could use to choose the right CMP:

Question	Scalr	ManageIQ	vRA	OneOps
Unique Selling Proposition	Resource Scaling, Budget Control	Continuous Discovery - IT Asset Management	Workflow Engine and Extensibility	DevOps Model of Management
License	Enterprise (Scalr)	OpenSource/ Enterprise (RedHat)	Enterprise (VMware)	OpenSource (Walmart)
Supported Virtualizations and Cloud	VMware, KVM, Hyper-V, OpenStack, AWS, Azure, and so on	VMware, OpenStack, AWS, Azure, GCP, and so on	VMware, OpenStack, AWS, Azure, Hyper-V	OpenStack, AWS, Azure, GCP, and so on
RBAC	Yes	Yes	Yes	Yes

Refer to the following link for a full and independent review of the CMPs: https://www.whatmatrix.com/comparison/Cloud-Management-Platforms#

General architecture of CMP

There are several CMPs on the market with varied architectures. However, there are some common principles that CMPs seem to follow for the most part:

- The highest common factor principle of CMP
    - The features available in CMP are normally the highest common denominator that is available to the varied clouds. This principle allows ease of development but does take a toll on the richness of the platform.
    - There may be some exceptions to this rule; if only a single cloud provides a certain feature, then that feature is allowed

- The CMP has its own abstraction and terminology
    - Each cloud uses its own terminology. For example, a region, availability zone (in AWS), data centers (Azure), and so on. In order to abstract these, the CMPs introduce their own terminology and sometimes create a map of the platforms in order to utilize them.
- CMPs integrate with the **CRUD** (**Create, Read, Update, and Delete**) APIs of the platform (AWS, Azure, GCP, OpenStack, and so on).
    - The CMPs mainly act like a provisioning engine (or at least, that's where they started - an exception to this is Manage IQ, which started as a CMDB/Asset Manager) and hence they focus on CRUD operations and the integration effort is focused on it.
- The CMPs expose their own APIs
    - Call it the current generation coding principle, or a way to allow other enterprise applications to connect to the system. The CMPs have their own APIs that are separate to the platforms (they mainly use REST as well).
- The CMPs are built in the infrastructure up mode
    - The CMPs are traditionally created in the Infrastructure Up mode, and hence the smallest unit that is normally received from them is a virtual machine and their associated entities (disks, networks, IPs, and so on)
- The CMPs may involve a workflow engine
    - The CMPs more often than not imbibe a workflow engine in order to allow for integrations.

ManageIQ

ManageIQ is an open source product that was created by Red Hat in 2014. Red Hat also uses CloudForms in its enterprise offerings. It was created from a CMDB/asset management mindset, and hence this product's most important aspect is its ability to discover the different cloud platforms.

You can deploy the open source version, ManageIQ, or the enterprise version, CloudForms (which has a few more additional features). The deployment can be done by using appliances or containers. It supports a simple and distributed installation to suit the needs of an enterprise.

Our motive is not to get into the different modes of deployment, but simply understand the architecture principles that are useful for our hybrid cloud.

ManageIQ is an orchestrator, which is a fancy way of saying it needs other system managers to function properly. We shall see that as we go further in the chapter. ManageIQ essentially performs three functions:

- Self-service
    - Ability for users to provision resources
- Compliance enforcement
    - Enforce controls in order to make the system compliant to legislation/standards such as HIPAA, PCI, SOX, and so on
- Optimization
    - This allows us to perform tasks such as right sizing the virtual machine, and so on

The system is created in Ruby on Rails. Since the system can be installed in a distributed environment, the system may also contain several appliances of ManageIQ performing different roles that come together as a CMP.

There are several roles that ManageIQ provides:

- Workers
- User interfaces
- Web services
- Automation
- Database
- Scheduling
- Reporting
- Notifier

Now you can see, that if the reporting load is high, we simply increase the nodes that are carrying the reporting role. If we need to add more concurrent users, the UI and web services roles can be scaled.

In order to be able to properly scale (with all these different roles), ManageIQ groups its appliances into zones and regions. The following diagram will help us understand the concept a little better:

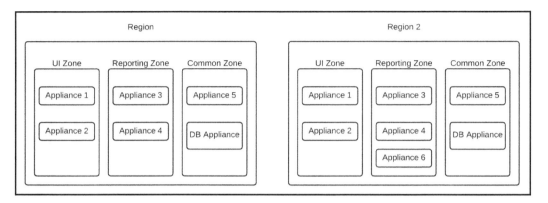

A **zone** is a cluster of appliances performing a similar function. We could create the zones as per our needs. Some companies even keep a zone per cloud platform they are managing and some keep it based on the role that they play (as shown in the above diagram).

A **region** on the other hand is a collection of zones, where a common database is used. In normal architecture, the region should be kept in the same physical region where the cloud provider is so as to minimize (and even protect) the traffic going out of the region.

Installing ManageIQ

The full range of installation options can be found in the ManageIQ documentation located at: `http://manageiq.org/docs/get-started/`. However, we are going to see a sample installation to see the concepts of the Hybrid Cloud in order.

We will be running a single instance of ManageIQ as a container in a Docker environment. In order to install **Docker** on any Linux machine, we follow the instructions in the next section. We can do this on any Linux machine even a virtual machine on the AWS (or any other) public cloud itself. However, in our case, we will be installing it on our management server.

 Please remember that since ManageIQ is a CMP, it will need API access (over HTTP(s)) to the clouds that we intend to manage with this CMP.

Preparing the host environment

The host environment that we are going to use to run Docker will be a Ubuntu 16.04 LTS virtual machine with about 4 GB RAM and 60 GB storage. In a production environment, we will need to size the host based on the requirements of the containers that need running.

Also, let's take a look at the basics of *containerization* itself before we take it any further.

Containerization basics

Containers are the natural evolution in terms of virtualization. As we all know, in the early days, we used to run the application on bare-metal servers. This led to a lot of resources being used, as the server was always sized for peak load and then some (*think the engineers safety margin rule*).

Then came along virtualization (without delving into the details of full-virtualization, para-virtualization, and hardware assisted virtualization), which simply added a layer (called the **Hypervisor**) atop the hardware that allowed multiple operating systems to use the abstracted hardware.

This hypervisor was actually a special operating system in itself, and like any regular OS, it had kernel and user space programs. As time passed by and the technology evolved, this special operating system; the **Hypervisor**, got thinner (lighter) and less resource intensive, however it was still an overhead:

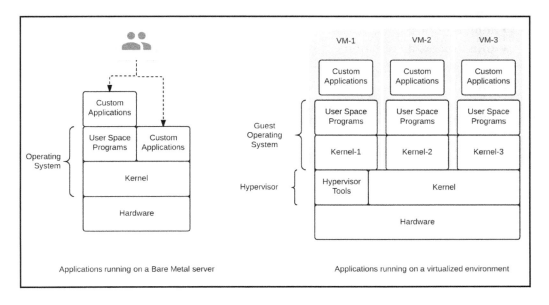

The preceding diagram depicts virtualization. As we can see, now we can run multiple, guest operating systems on the same hardware, thereby optimizing resource utilization.

In the preceding diagram, the hypervisor running atop the hardware signifies that it is a Type-1 hypervisor. There are several hypervisors, such as VMware Workstation, Virtual Box, or VMware Fusion, that run atop a full blown operating system - these are called Type-2 hypervisors.

Normally, a Type-2 hypervisor is used in a testing scenario and not in a production/enterprise setup.

So, all is well right? Well, we never can stop optimizing. So if you look at the preceding diagram, what do you see? Several instances of the **kernel**. Considering that all three virtual machines are running the same operating system, then the kernel will be the same. Which means we are running three copies of the same software. If only there was a way to isolate/instantiate the kernel and run multiple user space and custom applications atop that.

There is! It's called a **kernel namespace**. These were introduced in Linux Kernel version 2.4.19 in 2002. Yes, 15 years ago. This has led to the concept of containers. There are six major namespaces (or isolations) that the kernel can perform (and others in the works), they are as follows:

- **net**: Network isolation
- **user**: User isolation
- **mnt**: Mount point isolation
- **pid**: Process ID isolation
- **ipc**: Interprocess communication isolation
- **uts**: Allows different hostnames/domain names on the same host

I am sure you can now visualize how the applications running in the containers would look:

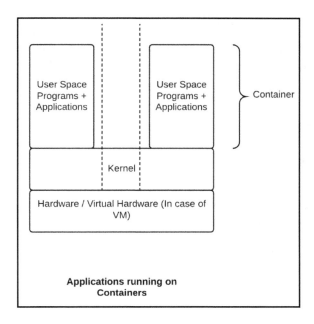

Applications running on Containers

If you are wondering how different this is from running multiple applications on a single operating system, just remember that each user space program is getting its own **slice** of the kernel and making modifications that don't disturb each other.

As you can see, we have removed as much overhead as possible while still retaining isolation. Another point that you must remember is that, since the containerization can happen at the kernel level, we can do it on the operating system installed on bare-metal directly, or on the OS that is running atop the hypervisor.

The only reason to run containerization atop a virtualized environment is because we need to run other operating systems that don't use the same kernel.

The Linux Kernel is the same for most distributions of Linux such as RedHat, Ubuntu, CentOS, Suse, and so on. So, if we want to run any of the distros in container mode, they can be done so on the same kernel.

When we mentioned the OS not using the same kernel, we were pointing at Windows, Unix, and so on.

It will be no surprise to you that in Windows Server 2016 onwards, Microsoft has launched a "micro-kernel" concept, which will help in containerizing the Windows applications and workloads.

Understanding and installing Docker

So, the ability to do containerization is over 15 years old, but why has it become famous only recently? It's because Docker (www.docker.com) has simplified it to the point where it only takes a few commands to create these namespaces and connect them in a usable manner.

Docker is an application that works on a *client-server* model. The Docker client helps us execute commands to the Docker server in order to control the containers. The Docker server itself runs on the kernel and creates the namespaces and connects them.

The images that are used by Docker are of the QCOW2 format—which makes it easier for us to layer images atop each other. The Docker images are normally stored in the public Docker repository. We can also choose to make our own private Docker repository within the enterprise for our allowed images and versions.

> **Copy On Write** (**COW**) format is where the underlying layer is not modified, but a top writable layer is provided. Any place where the block needs to be modified is written on the writable layer.
>
> This allows us to reuse the underlying layer several times over, without copying it. If you are familiar with VMware virtualization, it's a similar concept to a linked clone.
>
> The following diagram elucidates the concept. If the block has been written on the writable layer, that data is used, else the data from the main layer is used:

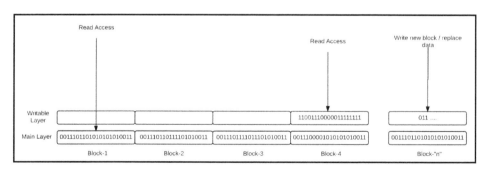

The Docker installation itself is fairly simple. Once a supported OS is installed, follow the directions for the same. Since we have used Ubuntu 16.04 LTS, the following commands can be used to install Docker.

The steps are simple:

1. Add the GPG key for the Docker repository to the system (to trust it).
2. Add the repository and update it.
3. Install the `docker-ce` (Docker Container Engine) package:

```
curl -fsSL https://download.docker.com/linux/ubuntu/gpg | sudo apt-key add -

sudo add-apt-repository "deb [arch=amd64]
https://download.docker.com/linux/ubuntu $(lsb_release -cs) stable"

sudo apt-get update

sudo apt-get install -y docker-ce
```

The preceding commands will install Docker on your system. Once installed, Docker is ready for us to use.

The Docker client can connect only from the `root` context. If you want to be able to run Docker commands without using `sudo`, then we can add a user to the Docker group by typing the following command:

```
sudo usermod -aG docker <enter your username here>
```

Once Docker is installed, we can now pull down images from the public repository and run them in various modes. You need to be cognizant of the fact that, by design, the Docker images are versioned and we have to specify the version of the image that we want to pull down. (Hint: *latest* version is normally the tag for the most updated version).

In order to check the installation, please execute the `hello-world` container using the following command:

```
docker run hello-world
```

Once you key the command in, the following takes place:

- Docker checks the local image repository for an image called `hello-world` (latest version is assumed)
- Since it doesn't find it, it tries to connect to the internet and download the Docker image
- After downloading the image, Docker runs an instance of it in a container (after creating all the required namespaces)
- Once the executable in the Docker image completes, the container is archived

> Docker is an application containerization platform, which means the container only has a reason to exist if an application is running. When the reason to exist disappears, so does the container.
>
> Each image is normally configured with the default application that it has to run (which can be overridden). This application receives "PID 1" inside the container, and just like the Linux machine, if "PID 1" dies, the system is shutdown.

Installing a ManageIQ container

Once Docker has been installed, the ManageIQ container is a matter of pulling the image and instantiating it:

```
sudo systemctl start docker

sudo docker run --privileged -d -p 8443:443 manageiq/manageiq:fine-4
```

The `docker run` command will pull all images of the ManageIQ fine-4 version, run it in a disconnect mode (`-d`), and map the port in the container HTTPS to the `8443` port on the container host (`-p 8443:443`).

```
alokshrivastwa@docker-container:~$ sudo systemctl start docker
alokshrivastwa@docker-container:~$ sudo docker run --privileged -d -p 8443:443 manageiq/manageiq:fine-4
Unable to find image 'manageiq/manageiq:fine-4' locally
fine-4: Pulling from manageiq/manageiq
d9aaf4d82f24: Pull complete
3a98b1e75e13: Pull complete
369d6a7661a2: Pull complete
a3a88482c019: Pull complete
8d3c7b3643c2: Pull complete
4053b833a3d5: Pull complete
54a8b0d192c5: Pull complete
ca16b4c9e859: Pull complete
dd826b647530: Pull complete
0fe365a68ccf: Pull complete
7b1026d478b3: Pull complete
0997e0c83efa: Pull complete
37c019a71c82: Pull complete
7c7d104276f1: Pull complete
Digest: sha256:42d22881999fb968a910cd48e2e8c43d2644f08ab34f91c0312bc84e26322159
Status: Downloaded newer image for manageiq/manageiq:fine-4
ece3764c03049b95587f95f073cfbe5fc2e688034556a19414529a9490e0faf0
alokshrivastwa@docker-container:~$
```

We can now log into the web UI of the Manage IQ system, by using the following link:

```
https://<IP address of Ubuntu16.04>:8443
```

The user credentials are `admin` and `smartvm`. You should remember that the server will have a self signed certificate, and so we will get a certificate error in the browser.

By default, we find that the server attaches itself to a default region and zone (**Region 0** and **Zone: default**):

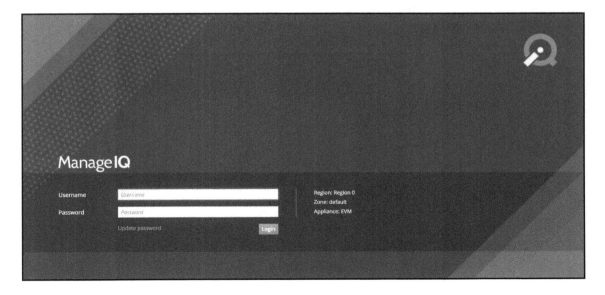

Configuring ManageIQ to connect to AWS and OpenStack

ManageIQ, or any similar orchestration platform will communicate with the underlying cloud using API keys. These come in different forms depending on the cloud provider.

For example, for AWS, it's an access key and secret key (akin to a username/password combination). For GCP, we have a `policy.json` file, and OpenStack, uses a username and password of a user defined in keystone.

Whatever it might be, it is simply a way to authenticate calls that are being made to the platform. In this case, we will just add the infrastructure providers in the ManageIQ tool.

Adding a new AWS EC2 provider

Perform the following steps:

1. Go to **Compute** | **Clouds** | **Provider**.
2. Click on **Add a new Cloud Provider**.
3. Type in a **Name** (this is only for the tool and should make sense to you).
4. Choose the **Type** as **Amazon EC2.**
5. Choose the **Region**.
6. Enter the **Access Key** and **Secret Key.**
7. Click on **Validate**.

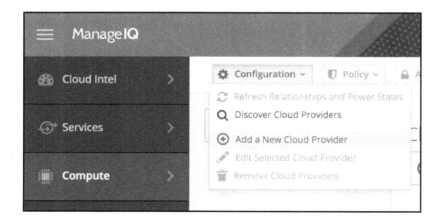

Now for the most important question, where do we get the access key and secret key from? If you remember, we created a user in the AWS console and we chose to give a user API access. You will find that it generates the access key and a secret key.

> It's a good idea to create a different user for use with an orchestrator, so that the API calls made by it can be appropriated.

If you don't remember, worry not. Log in to your AWS console, by going to `https://aws.amazon.com/`.

Once you log in, go to the IAM service and click on **Users** | **Add User**:

1. Give it a **User name**
2. Select the **Programmatic access**
3. Click on **Next**
4. Click **add user** to the group
5. If the group doesn't exist, create a new one using the following steps:
    1. Give it a **Group name.**
    2. Click on **Administrative Access** - please remember that we are choosing Admin access for ease of deployment, in a real-life production environment, it should be a finely-tuned policy.
6. Finally **review** and click on **Create user**:

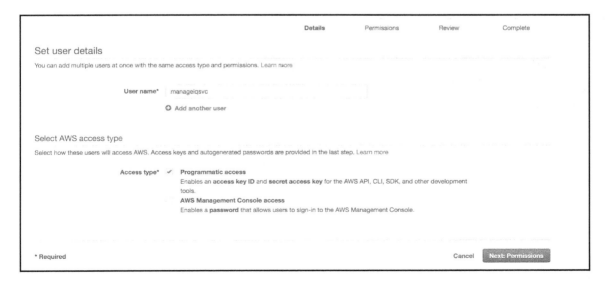

You can see the **Access Key** and **Secret Key** that you have to add to the ManageIQ endpoint.

 In a testing environment, it is okay to provide **Administrative access** to the service user we have created. But in production, please fine-tune the policy to allow access to the user only for the services that it needs to.

Once the validation is successful in the ManageIQ engine, please scroll down and click on **Add**. ManageIQ can now discover all the things that are running on the system:

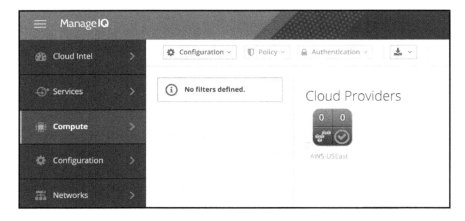

In this case, since nothing is running, it shows nothing. But the green check mark means that it was able to successfully connect to the cloud.

Adding our OpenStack endpoint

The addition of OpenStack is the same as the AWS endpoint, but in this case, we need a minimum of three details:

- Keystone URL
    - If Keystone version 3 is used, then we need the domain name, as the server supports multi-domain authentication
    - The port to be used is also from
- Region name
- Username
- Password

This information can be found in our OpenStack installation. In our case, the DevStack installation. We can simply log in to the OpenStack dashboard (see the previous chapter, where we installed the DevStack environment for the login details) and navigate to **Identity | Users** and click on **Create User**.

We can see the user domain name in this screen:

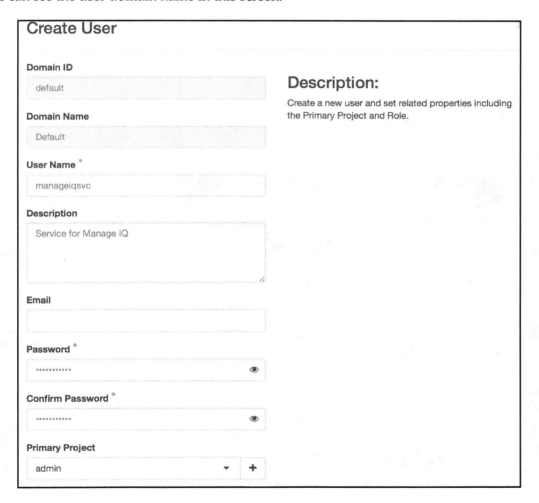

Once created, log out and log in with the new user. Once you are logged in, click on the user name on the right and click on download the RC file. This file will have all the information for us to be able to use the API of OpenStack:

Download the RC file v3 for Keystone version 3. Once you open the file, you can see the username, the region name, and the Keystone port from the URL (if no port is mentioned, it's the default port for the protocol - HTTP 80, HTTPS 443). The following image shows the required info marked with white rectangles:

```
export OS_AUTH_URL=http://10.128.0.3/identity/v3

# With the addition of Keystone we have standardized on the term **project**
# as the entity that owns the resources.
export OS_PROJECT_ID=efd386f32eb64748981e01dbb0ae203b
export OS_PROJECT_NAME="admin"
export OS_USER_DOMAIN_NAME="Default"
if [ -z "$OS_USER_DOMAIN_NAME" ]; then unset OS_USER_DOMAIN_NAME; fi

# unset v2.0 items in case set
unset OS_TENANT_ID
unset OS_TENANT_NAME

# In addition to the owning entity (tenant), OpenStack stores the entity
# performing the action as the **user**.
export OS_USERNAME="manageiqsvc"

# With Keystone you pass the keystone password.
echo "Please enter your OpenStack Password for project $OS_PROJECT_NAME as user $OS_USERNAME: "
read -sr OS_PASSWORD_INPUT
export OS_PASSWORD=$OS_PASSWORD_INPUT

# If your configuration has multiple regions, we set that information here.
# OS_REGION_NAME is optional and only valid in certain environments.
export OS_REGION_NAME="RegionOne"
# Don't leave a blank variable, unset it if it was empty
if [ -z "$OS_REGION_NAME" ]; then unset OS_REGION_NAME; fi

export OS_INTERFACE=public
export OS_IDENTITY_API_VERSION=3
```

In this case, we have:

- **Username**: `manageiqsvc`
- **Password**: <The password we set while creating the user>
- **Keystone URL**: `http://10.128.0.3/identity/v3`
- **Keystone Port**: 80 (default for HTTP)
- **Region Name**: `RegionOne`
- **Keystone Version**: 3

With this information, we can add the endpoint to the ManageIQ system.

Provisioning virtual machines using ManageIQ

Once ManageIQ has been configured with the endpoints, we can simply start using it to create machines in AWS and OpenStack. Remember that the architectural significance of this will be dealt with later in the chapter. Let's see how we can create a Catalog Item, which can be published to the users in order to create virtual machines on both clouds from a single pane of glass.

You need to remember that a Catalog, not only has the base details, but is also the system that ties the configuration management systems and automation together:

In the case, we simply want to provision a virtual machine without creating a catalog, we can do so by navigating to **Compute | Cloud | Instances**:

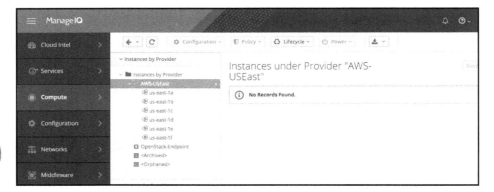

Once there, we can Click on **Lifecycle -> Provision Instance**

Select the image you want to provision. Please remember, that by default public images on AWS will not be shown, unless the filters are set to allow it.

You will find your AWS private images and OpenStack images, select one to provision and click **Next**.

Fill in the details (**Instance Name**, **Instance Type**, and so on) and click **Submit**. You can see the instance in the OpenStack environment.

Creating a catalog

To create a catalog we need to know four things:

1. A *Catalog* is used to show the Catalog Items to the user.
2. A *Service Dialog* is used to get any inputs from the user.
3. An *Automation Workflow* is used to provision workflow.
4. A *Catalog Item* ties the service dialog and the automation workflow together and is a part of the Catalog.

Creating a Service Dialog

A Service Dialog and Automation Workflow are a part of Automation, and are required if we need the catalog item to be seen in the Catalog.

1. Navigate to **Automation** | **Automate** | **Customization**
2. Click on **Service Dialog, Choose Configuration**, and Add a new Service Dialog, Once the service Dialog is added, we can then add the new tab, and finally a new element in the tab:

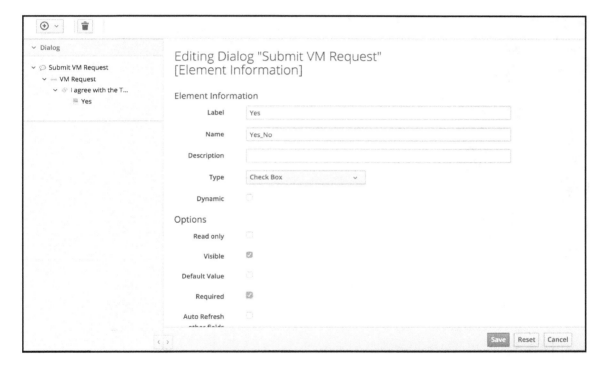

 Although we are not doing anything with this checkbox yet, we can configure this to pass the user variables to the automation workflows.

Creating a catalog item and catalog

A catalog is what we expose to the end users, so that they can request for resources. The catalog can have several catalog items in them. In order to create them, please follow the instructions below.

1. Navigate to **Services** | **Catalog**, click on **Catalog Items** on the left. Click on **Configuration** | **Add a new Catalog Item**. Choose the **Catalog Item Type** as **OpenStack**:

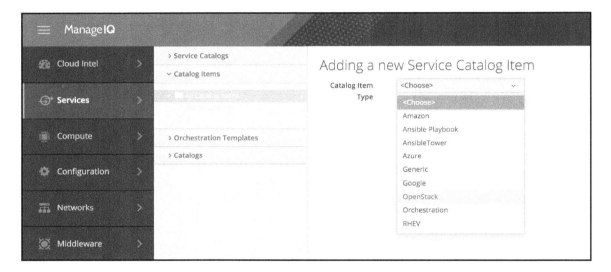

2. Once done, we will be presented with a form, where we provide a **Name/Description** under the **Basic Info**. Choose the created **Dialog**:

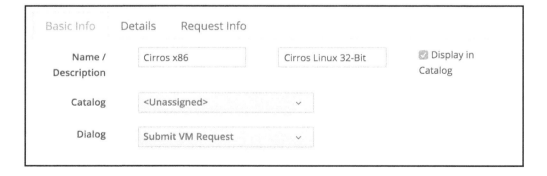

3. On the **Request Info** button, choose the **Image**, and select the **Instance name** (under **Catalog**), **Instance type** (under **Properties**), **Cloud Network** and **Tenant** (under **Environment**). We can choose to add the other details if needed. Click on **Add**:

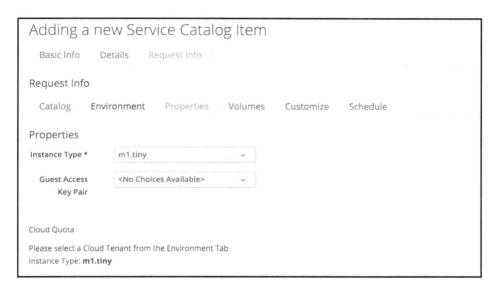

4. Select the catalogs from the menu, click on **Configuration**, click on **Add new catalog**. Give it a name, and then select the catalog item created:

Testing the catalog

Now the catalog is ready to request. In order to test it, click on **Services | Catalogs**, choose **Service Catalogs** and click on **Catalog Item** and click on **Order**. We will be asked dialog questions (in our case, we have created a terms and conditions checkbox earlier):

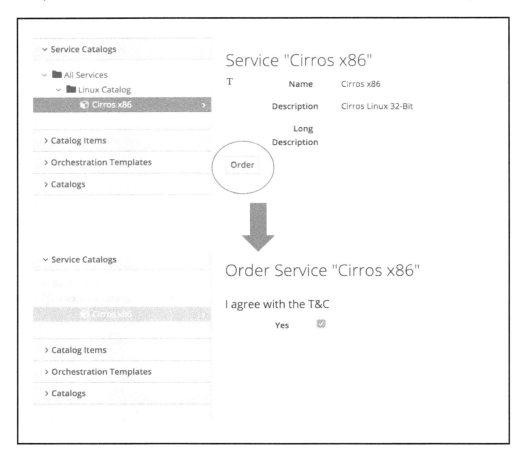

Once we submit the request, the system will request the resources from the respective cloud (in our case, the OpenStack environment):

You can also see that the name of the instance has the same prefix that we mentioned while creating the catalog item.

A detailed document describing the automation configuration of ManageIQ can be found at: `https://www.gitbook.com/book/pemcg/mastering-automation-in-cloudforms-4-2-and-manage/details`

Policies and user authentication

The ManageIQ system allows us to specify the policies for both compliance and control of your virtual environment that will be provisioned by the system.

The compliance policies deal with the hardening of systems to be in compliance with regulatory bodies such as HIPAA, SOX, and so on. Control on the other hand, is more event-based, and allows us to take action if a certain event happens.

The system also allows integration with OpenSCAP. The details about these integrations are beyond the purview of the book and it is sufficient to understand that these capabilities can be used when needed.

Refer to the following link in order to understand this in detail: `http://manageiq.org/docs/reference/latest/doc-Policies_and_Profiles_Guide/miq/`

ManageIQ also allows us to integrate the authentication with Microsoft Active directory, SAML, 2FA, and so on. Please read the following link in order to know more: `http://manageiq.org/docs/reference/latest/auth/active_directory`

Creating cloud images

Creating images has been at the core of infrastructure automation. I am sure we have all created or at least used virtual machine images. It is one of the major reasons for the rise of the adoption of virtualization: its ease of management.

The cloud also uses images, as one of the underlying technologies is virtualization. Now, for the most important question, *"how different is the image created for the cloud from one created for virtualization?"* The answer is, *"Not much!"*

The cloud uses known (sometimes modified/tweaked) versions of the virtualization platforms that we have already worked on. As an example, AWS uses a modified version of Xen. OpenStack can technically work with any hypervisor, but the choice is normally KVM. Azure would work with Hyper-V.

This means that creating cloud images will not be very different from what we have been doing so far in order to create the corresponding virtualization images. We may need to change the format of the image (similar when migrating from a VMware ESXi to Hyper-V) as different hypervisors need different formats.

However, there needs to be some additional software installed on the images. This will allow the cloud to run post-provisioning tasks. The software that we are talking about is **cloud-init** (`https://cloud-init.io`). This particular system is used to read the metadata that is injected in the cloud images and perform the post provisioning tasks. These tasks include but are not limited to:

- Injecting the SSH public key to allow login to the servers (Linux)
- Setting up the administrator passwords (Windows)
- Installing the agents of configuration management tools such as Chef and Puppet and bootstrapping them
- Setting the host name on the server

The other changes that we need to make on the image while making a cloud ready is to remove any sort of remaining and un-needed data in the network configuration - such as statically defining the MAC address, and so on.

There are many ways that one could go about creating images in the cloud, let's take a look at the two primary ones:

- Convert an existing virtual machine image into the cloud image
- Clone/copy a cloud image and modify it to suit your needs

For the first one, most public clouds normally provide a way to upload an already existing OVF (Open Virtualization Format), VMDK (Virtual Machine Disk - VMware), VHD (Virtual Hard Disk - Hyper-V), and so on to the cloud image. Please remember that we may have to install cloud-init prior to the conversion.

As an example, AWS has a service called VM Import/Export that we can use to import the virtual machine images from a wide variety of formats to be converted to the AMI (Amazon Machine Image). For more information refer to: `http://docs.aws.amazon.com/vm-import/latest/userguide/vmimport-image-import.html`

However, when it comes to private clouds such as OpenStack's private implementation, we simply have to install the tools required (cloud-init) and convert it to the right image format. A good tool for the job is to use the OpenSource **qemu-img**. This can convert between qcow2, vhd, vmdk, and raw formats. Read the following man page for the options (`http://manpages.ubuntu.com/manpages/xenial/man1/qemu-img.1.html`).

The second methodology is made possible because of the principle operating system manufacturers creating a base image of their operating systems for the cloud. We can simply create a virtual machine from these base images, add our own packages, and convert them into our own private templates (or even public ones). This method can be performed manually, or by using a tool that HashiCorp (`https://www.hashicorp.com`) has created called **Packer** (`https://www.packer.io/`).

In this chapter, we will simply understand the core concepts of Packer. Packer technically has only three important core concepts to understand (there are some auxiliary ones that are not covered later):

- Builders
- Provisioners
- Post-processors

The way Packer works is that it needs a base image that we would specify, the builder would create a virtual machine in the given cloud, and the post provisioner performs installation and configuration of the software that we need to add atop the base image. This is then converted to the new cloud image.

Post-provisioners are optional and are used for purposes such as copying the images to different locations and so on. The following flowchart shows the use of Packer in order to create the images:

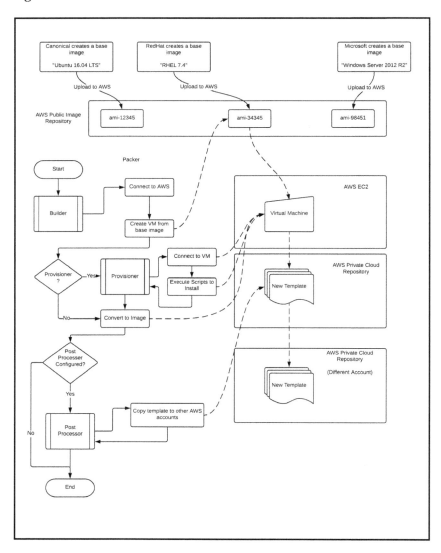

In the preceding image, the **Public Cloud Repository** and **Private Cloud Repository** are shown for learning purposes only, they are technically AMIs that are tagged with public/private and stored in S3.

While the example in this case has been given using AWS, Packer works with a wide variety of public clouds, private clouds, and even virtualized data centers.

The entire Packer file is written as JSON and so it can be versioned, managed, and treated as code. The following example shows a Packer configuration for AWS:

```
{
  "variables": {
  "aws_access_key": "",
  "aws_secret_key": ""
  },
  "builders": [{
  "type": "amazon-ebs",
  "access_key": "{{user `aws_access_key`}}",
  "secret_key": "{{user `aws_secret_key`}}",
  "region": "us-west-1",
  "source_ami": "ami-12345",
  "instance_type": "t1.small",
  "ssh_username": "ec2-user",
  "ami_name": "packer-test {{timestamp}}"
  }],

  "provisioners": [
  {
  "type": "shell",
  "inline": [
  "sudo apt-get install -y git",
  "ssh-keyscan github.com >> ~/.ssh/known_hosts"
  ]
  }
```

Packer will use the AWS access and secret key to connect. It will then take the source AMI (ami-12345), spin up an instance of size t1.small, install GIT and add the GitHub key as a known host, and convert it into an AMI known as packer-test (appended with the time stamp of when Packer has run).

For more information on how to use Packer, please see the documentation on the website mentioned earlier in the section.

In conclusion – architecting with a CMP

All of the previous information leads us to this topic. So, when should we use a CMP and what should we use it for? What use cases does it solve? Let's take a quick look at these one more time:

When should we use a CMP?

- When we need a *Single Pane of Glass* approach
- When we need a similar automation framework requirement in all the clouds
- When we intend to start the life cycle at the provisioning of the workload
- When the major workloads are virtual machines and IaaS components (and not PaaS)
- When we need a single abstraction for the clouds
- When we need to minimize the learning curve for the current IT staff (the CMP itself will be an additional management overhead)

Which CMP should we use?

This question needs to take a lot of parameters into consideration. As a first step, please use the comparison tool link provided earlier in this chapter. That will provide the compatibility matrix and features.

The other choice that we have to make is between the open source or the COTS application. Consider the support and knowledge levels of your current staff, as well as lock-in and the features that it provides before taking a decision in this respect.

When NOT to use a CMP-based cloud

- When we need to use advanced services (PaaS, containers, serverless, cognitive, and so on)
- When we need to use the supporting application use case - the CMP will be an overkill and possibly not add any value
- When we need multiple modes of provisioning and not only through the CMP

I hope this sets the architecture considerations for the CMPs for a hybrid cloud straight. We need to be cognizant of the fact that without extensibility, most CMPs will not perform infrastructure plumbing - which means that they will simply provision the resources and not connect them to each other in a logical manner. This might be useful in the case of cloud bursting.

Summary

In this chapter, we saw how to build a hybrid cloud that is created for the Supporting Applications Use Case and also the Isolated/Distributed Use Case with the help of a Cloud Management Platform (CMP). In the next chapter, we will build a hybrid cloud on the basis of containers and a container orchestrator, in which the infrastructure plumbing becomes easy.

7
Building a Containerized Hybrid Cloud

In the last chapter, we saw how to create a hybrid cloud using a **Cloud Management Platform** (**CMP**). I am sure you will agree, when I say that it would take a lot of infrastructure plumbing in order to use CMP mode for a cloud bursting use case.

 Infrastructure plumbing implies modification of configuration in various systems in order to enable communication between the application components.

It is definitely possible with CMP, although difficult, and one may need to integrate some code in order to make it work.

In the previous chapter, we also briefly touched upon containers while we were installing ManageIQ in a container. The containers are extremely portable and can run in any place the appropriate kernel is present.

There are two major container engines, Docker and Rocket (from Core OS). For a single container the management is very easy; however, once the scale increases, the need for an orchestration platform for containers becomes inevitable.

 At the time of writing the book, Red Hat are in talks with CoreOS to purchase them, so it may be possible that Rocket may be overshadowed by Project Atomic from Red Hat.

There are several systems that enable the orchestration of containers themselves. Some examples include Kubernetes (also called k8s, meaning helmsman, the person who steers a boat/ship), Docker Swarm, Apache Mesos, Red Hat OpenShift, among others.

Evolving to containers

While we have seen an isolated example of how we can use containers to deploy something very quickly, the most important thing is to understand the need and the ability to run the applications in containers.

Containers improve portability between the different environments and even different distributions of the OS, as long as we have a common kernel. Containers are also very light and can quickly be spun up and down. For these reasons, containers are the number one choice for developing modern applications with a microservice architecture.

Now, technically a container is a combination of the namespaces offered by the Linux Kernel (Windows containers with Docker for Windows were launched with Windows Server 2016, after introducing the microkernel for Windows).

The one major component in this is container networking, as the containers need to talk to each other. In the following section, let's talk about container networking, as this will be the underpinning service for a hybrid cloud based on containers.

Container networking

The most popular types of container networking are as follows:

- None—no networking
- Bridge networking
- Host networking
- Overlay networking
- Underlay networking

The list might look familiar to people with virtualization experience as the first three are extensively used in virtualized environments too.

None – no networking

This creates an isolated network namespace for the container with just a local loop-back adapter and no allocated external connection. This is used for testing containers. This feature is available in both Docker and Rocket.

Bridge networking

The bridged situation is normal for Docker. An internal bridge is created and all the containers share the bridge, which means they can communicate among themselves, however the IP address for the containers is not exposed to the outside.

From the outside, the container services can be mapped to the host using Network and Port Address Translation.

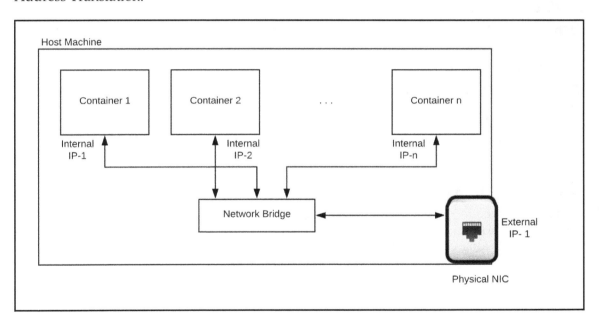

In the preceding figure, **Container 1** through **Container n** can all talk to each other. However, they cannot communicate externally, therefore, we expose the service through the Physical NIC using NAT.

Say **Container 1** and **Container 2** are both running a web server on port 80 and **Container n** is running a database on port 3306. We can expose this as follows:

Internal IP address and port	External IP address and port
Internal IP-1: 80	External IP-1:8080
Internal IP-2:80	External IP-1:8081
Internal IP-n:3306	External IP-1:3306

As you can see, the containers' ports are mapped to the host port, so internally they will still see port 80, but different ports are required to access them from outside.

Host networking

In this case, rather than creating a new network namespace, the namespace of the host where the containers are running is used. This provides immense data transfer speeds, but can cause port conflicts.

This is only used when we want to isolate the other namespaces but not the network. In the previous example, the container will have access to the full network stack of the host. This simply means that containers are like different applications running on the same host and no port duplication can be done.

Overlay networking

This is used to connect the different hosts together. We can run an overlay protocol, such as GRE, in order to connect the different hosts. There are several products that perform overlay networking in a container environment, for example Cisco ACI, Contriv, Flannel, and so on.

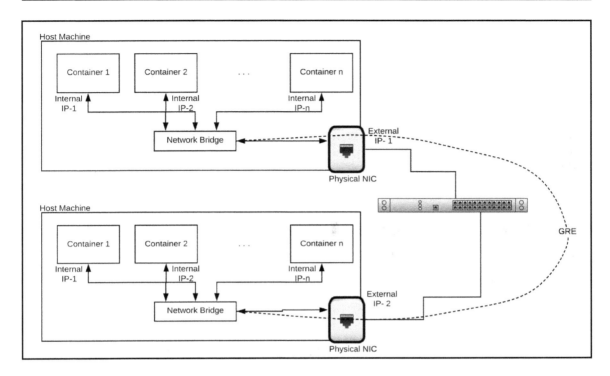

In the preceding diagram, you can see the overlay network (dotted line) running on the physical network (connected to the switch). This allows the network to be extended between multiple container hosts and makes communication possible.

Underlay networking

In this, the physical hardware is involved. This means the devices communicate with the physical switches and can create a VLAN so that the network is isolated. There are two types:

- MAC VLAN:

    In this, the containers take a new MAC address and an IP address (in the same subnet as the host interface) similar to the sub-interface concept in Cisco devices.

- IP VLAN:

    In this, the containers create sub-interfaces, but they can be on a completely different physical VLANs. This means the switches will need to be informed about them, and therefore a system that can orchestrate the physical switches are needed.

Since the underlay network requires the modifications be done on the physical network layer, it's not used frequently in enterprise environments, as a lot of the switches may be old and therefore unsupported.

Container orchestration engine

The following are the major container orchestration engines:

- Kubernetes (k8s)
- Mesos
- Swarm

In this book, we will be dealing with Kubernetes mainly. We expect the following features:

- Ability to provision/deprovision containers across multiple hosts
- Ability to connect storage and network to the containers
- Ability to route requests to the containers

Almost all the platforms provide this, however, let's take a look at Kubernetes and how it provides these features. The reason we choose Kubernetes as an example is because it has been adopted more widely than any other competitor on the market, and some cloud providers even support it directly. For example, Azure has an ACE (Azure Container Engine) based on Kubernetes and Red Hat's OpenShift platform uses Kubernetes as the underlying system.

Kubernetes architecture

Kubernetes is a system that works on the concept of a cluster. A Kubernetes cluster has two categories of nodes. These are `master` and `worker` (a.k.a. minion).

The `master` node in Kubernetes runs three core services:

- `kube-apiserver`: This service provides API access for the master, so we can communicate with it using the `kubectl` command

- `kube-controller-manager`: This is the heart of the system and manages the activities done by Kubernetes

- `kube-scheduler`: As the name implies, it finds the proper location (host) and has enough resources for the containers can run

The `worker` node on the other hand has two services:

- `kubelet`: This is a Kubernetes agent that talks to the master node (it also communicates with the `kube-apiserver`)

- `kube-proxy`: This service takes care of networking, as it is a networking proxy

The following diagram shows the preceding architecture with the previously mentioned components:

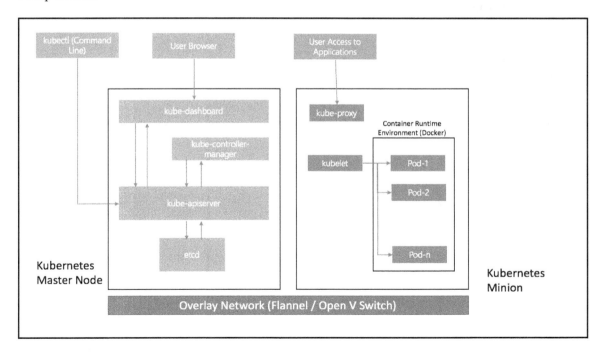

In a real-world scenario, the cluster is highly available from a controller (master node) standpoint and the **minions** are increased as the need for capacity increases.

 The most important decision to make when setting up Kubernetes for a Hybrid Cloud scenario is to choose the overlay network layer, as choosing a network layer which may not be supported by all the Infrastructure providers will break the inter-cluster communication. Also, Kubernetes will have a cluster federation feature, which will allow us to build the Hybrid Cloud.

Basic concepts in Kubernetes

Now that we have seen the architecture of Kubernetes, let's take a look at some of the basic terminology and concepts that will help us later in deployment, and start using the Kubernetes Container Orchestration System.

These are the basic things that we need to understand about Kubernetes:

- Pod
- Controllers
- Service
- Volumes
- Namespace

Pod

A **pod** is the smallest unit in the world of Kubernetes. It represents a single unit of deployment in Kubernetes. It is a combination of:

- One or more containers
- Storage resources
- Network IP address

If there is more than one container in a pod, they communicate among themselves using the `localhost` address (and of course, different ports on different containers) and can share a volume.

Controllers

Controllers typically manage the pods, and their creation, replication, roll outs, and so on. Controllers are of different kinds and the important ones are as follows:

- ReplicaSet/replication controller:
    - Runs a specified number of pods at any given point in time. Most Highly Available (HA) applications would use these, such as web servers and so on.
- Stateful set:
    - These are used for the applications that need to maintain state. This provides persistent storage, networking, and so on. It's useful when running databases and so on.
- Daemon set controllers:
    - Used to create the pods in all the minions that are added. For instance, when we need to run a certain application on every minion node, for example, monitoring / log collection agents such as logstash, and distributed file systems such as glusterfs/ceph, and so on.
- Deployment controllers:
    - Once the deployment is created, the deployment controller monitors the state of deployment and takes action as necessary.

So, if an application is running in a pod on a minion and the minion goes down, if configured in the deployment, the system will bring up a new pod on the surviving minions.

Service

Service is Kubernetes' way of exposing the pods for incoming traffic. The service basically accepts the traffic and routes them to the pods. The services don't change as the pods are added/removed. In addition to providing the inbound connections, they also provide load balancing and DNS services to the pod.

Volumes

If you have worked with containers, we know that when a container is started, it starts with a clean slate due to the underlying *Copy on Write* mechanism, which means that the files are ephemeral and are not stored normally.

This can become a problem when the pod is running multiple containers, or when the pod is running software such as a database. In these cases, the data needs to be persisted across the creation and deletion of not only containers but pods too.

In order to solve this, Kubernetes has volumes (a very similar concept to Docker, but more tightly managed in comparison). The Kubernetes system creates persistent volumes that are then exposed to the pods.

Kubernetes supports the following for persistent storage (non-exhaustive list):

- AWS EBS
- Azure Disk
- Azure File
- Ceph
- GCE (Google Container Engine) Persistent Disk
- iSCSI
- NFS
- Fiber Channel
- vSphere Volume

 You can refer to `https://kubernetes.io/docs/concepts/storage/volumes/` for the supported devices.

When a pod is created with a persistent volume, Kubernetes uses one of the systems to store the data so that the volumes are persisted.

Namespaces

Namespaces allows us to run multiple virtual Kubernetes clusters on the same physical cluster, thereby allowing the same names of systems in different namespaces.

If you are wondering where this might be useful, consider a scenario where a central IT team has deployed a cluster that is used by multiple project teams. Now, two teams can't create the same pod name if we did not have namespaces. We could also provide a quota for namespaces.

At the time of writing this book, Kubernetes is not served as an SaaS platform. This means we need multiple deployments of Kubernetes for serving multiple customers, as it doesn't have the required RBAC. If that is the need, Red Hat OpenShift adds it for Kubernetes.

The following diagram should help in understanding all the different components that were discussed previously:

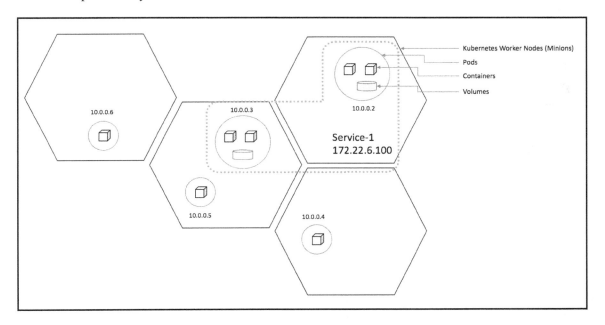

The preceding figure shows the concepts in a **k8s** cluster. The hexagons are the **Worker** nodes. The circles in them are different pods. The cubes are the containers where the business logic/code runs. If there are a number of them, then a persistent volume is attached. Note that there is no reason why **Volumes** cannot be used in a *single* container pod. The preceding diagram was shown for representative purposes only.

A group of pods are exposed to the world with a service. Note the IP addresses that are shown, the controllers are not shown in the diagram as they simply monitor and manage the pods. Kubelet and Kube-Proxy are also not shown but they will be present on all the nodes.

So in this case, the **user** will connect to 172.22.6.100, then the service will internally send the request to one of the pods, and the containers will process the request.

Kubernetes deployment

There are several ways we can deploy Kubernetes, some of which are suitable for production use and some of them are simply for testing.

 Refer to the following link to check the right solution for you when deploying a Kubernetes cluster: `https://kubernetes.io/docs/setup/pick-right-solution/`

In this book however, we will use Juju from Canonical in order to help deploy the Kubernetes cluster. We will simply see how to deploy a production grade cluster with the appropriate Juju charm, and then we will deploy Kubefed to set up a federation among the clouds.

Introduction to Juju

Juju is an open source application modelling platform that works in multiple clouds. This tool aligns well with our use case as we are trying to deploy a Hybrid Cloud. Juju needs a machine that can act as a controller and we can deploy in-house. We may also choose to use a hosted model of Juju from Canonical, called JAAS (Juju as a Service).

Juju performs its actions with scripts called **charms**. The Juju charms are a set of scripts that deploy the software that we need. Charms are single pieces of software such as a HAProxy and so on. Several charms can be bundled together in a Juju bundle (for example, OpenStack, Kubernetes, and so on), and Juju can be used to perform the following functions on the applications:

- Install the software
- Configure the software (and dependencies/relationships)
- Upgrade/update the software
- Scale-in/out (add or remove more instances of the applications)

There are other features of the system such as bench-marking, performing operational tasks, and performing health checks.

 Refer to the link `https://jujucharms.com` to learn more about Juju charms and the different charms that are available for different software.

However, in this book we are more interested in deploying Kubernetes using Juju. The following table shows the different clouds that are supported by Juju for Kubernetes:

IaaS provider	Operating system	Networking support
AWS	Ubuntu	Flannel, Calico
OpenStack	Ubuntu	Flannel, Calico
Azure	Ubuntu	Flannel
Google Compute Engine	Ubuntu	Flannel
Joyent	Ubuntu	Flannel
Rackspace	Ubuntu	Flannel
vSphere	Ubuntu	Flannel, Calico

So, if we are using a combination of clouds, then using Juju is a no-brainer. Also, we can see that Flannel is the common networking system and is supported across all platforms, therefore our environment will use it.

Juju's architecture consists of a **client**, with which we perform functions, and a controller. The **controller** is created per infrastructure provider that we want to manage with the Juju system. If you have worked with a configuration management system, such as Chef, you would have seen the same architecture. The Juju client is akin to *knife* and the **controller** can be compared to *chef-server*.

As we mentioned, the controller is per cloud. This is because Juju performs additional features such as monitoring and so on. Juju also provides a dashboard, which we can use to model the different applications.

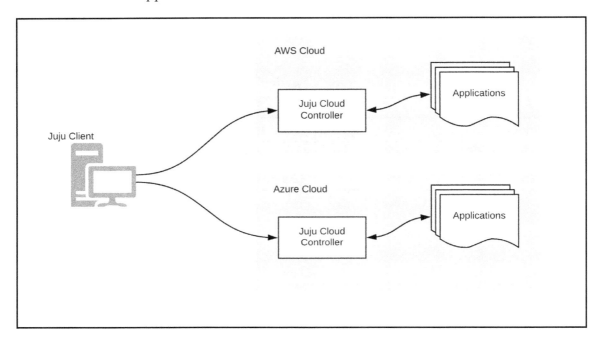

Installing the Juju client and bootstrapping clouds

As the first step of deploying Kubernetes, we will install the Juju client on the workstation or the management node. There are several operating systems that are supported for the Juju client. I will be installing it on the *Ubuntu workstation* that I use for cloud management. Please remember you can use your own workstation in order to deploy the client.

 In order to install it for Windows, CentOS, or Mac OSX, please visit the following link: https://jujucharms.com/docs/2.0/reference-releases.

The installation is simply a matter of adding the repository and installing Juju:

```
sudo add-apt-repository ppa:juju/stable
sudo apt update
sudo apt install juju
```

This will install the Juju client. Once complete, we will then bootstrap our AWS Cloud and then deploy the Juju controller over there. We will perform the same thing for our OpenStack Cloud. Once these are completed, we can then deploy Kubefed for the federations.

In order to see all the clouds that are supported by Juju, type the command `juju list-clouds`

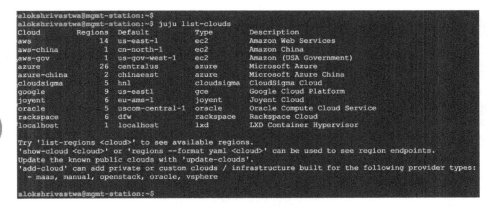

During the writing of this book, AWS, AWS GovCloud, Azure, Azure China, Cloud Sigma, Oracle, Google, Joyent, Rackspace, and so on are the current public cloud providers.

OpenStack and vSphere are among several private/custom clouds that are supported by the system.

As a next step, we will create the credentials that we will use with the AWS Cloud:

```
juju add-credential <cloud name>
```

We will add the access key and secret key that we have been using in all the other places:

```
alokshrivastwa@mgmt-station:~$ juju add-credential aws
Enter credential name: default-aws-creds

Using auth-type "access-key".

Enter access-key: AKIAIAYAET7L5FGKYONQ

Enter secret-key:

Credentials added for cloud aws.

alokshrivastwa@mgmt-station:~$ 
```

Depending on the cloud, the requested credentials will vary. For example, Google Cloud requires a JSON file.

In order to check the credentials already stored in Juju, we execute the following command:

```
juju list-credentials
```

The default credentials for a cloud have an asterisk (*) at their side. At this point, we will only see the `default-aws-credentials` that we have added in the preceding section:

```
alokshrivastwa@instance-1:~$ juju list-credentials
Cloud   Credentials
aws     default-aws-creds

alokshrivastwa@instance-1:~$ 
```

Bootstrapping an AWS Cloud

Once the credentials are stored, we have to create a controller in AWS in order to start using Juju. The command to bootstrap the AWS Cloud is as follows:

```
juju bootstrap <cloud> <controller name>
```

So, we will execute the script and wait for the controller to come online. In essence, the system makes an API call to the AWS Cloud to spin an instance, then connects to it, and finally runs configuration management to configure the instance:

```
alokshrivastwa@instance-1:~$ juju bootstrap aws my-aws-controller
Creating Juju controller "my-aws-controller" on aws/us-east-1
Looking for packaged Juju agent version 2.3.2 for amd64
Launching controller instance(s) on aws/us-east-1...
 - i-0a516544dabba7471 (arch=amd64 mem=4G cores=2)us-east-1a"
Installing Juju agent on bootstrap instance
Fetching Juju GUI 2.11.1
Waiting for address
Attempting to connect to 54.161.35.46:22
Attempting to connect to 172.31.19.61:22
Connected to 54.161.35.46
Running machine configuration script...
Bootstrap agent now started
Contacting Juju controller at 54.161.35.46 to verify accessibility...
Bootstrap complete, "my-aws-controller" controller now available
Controller machines are in the "controller" model
Initial model "default" added
alokshrivastwa@instance-1:~$
```

We can also see that in the AWS Cloud, a machine has been spun up:

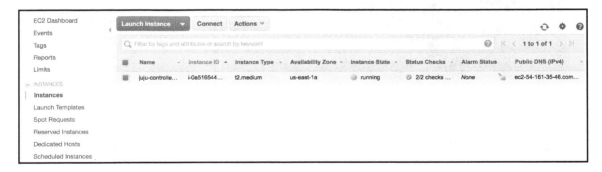

Now the Juju controller is ready to use and we can deploy Juju charms.

Bootstrapping an OpenStack Cloud

In Juju, we can bootstrap our OpenStack Cloud, however, we need to add it first using the following command:

```
juju add-cloud
```

We can then provide the Keystone details and add the credentials for the OpenStack Cloud:

```
alokshrivastwa@instance-1:~$ juju add-cloud
Cloud Types
  maas
  manual
  openstack
  oracle
  vsphere

Select cloud type: openstack

Enter a name for your openstack cloud: my-devstack

Enter the API endpoint url for the cloud: http://10.128.0.3:5000/v2

Auth Types
  access-key
  userpass

Select one or more auth types separated by commas: userpass

Enter region name: RegionOne

Enter the API endpoint url for the region [use cloud api url]:

Enter another region? (Y/n): n

Cloud "my-devstack" successfully added
You may bootstrap with 'juju bootstrap my-devstack'
alokshrivastwa@instance-1:~$
```

We will also add credentials and bootstrap it:

```
juju add-credential my-devstack
juju bootstrap my-devstack
```

Once the cloud is bootstrapped, you will see that the Juju controller is created on the OpenStack system as well.

Accessing the Juju controller using a GUI

The Juju controller comes with a dashboard that can be used to manage the Juju deployments. In order to see the controllers currently running, please execute the command, `juju list-controllers`:

```
alokshrivastwa@instance-1:~$ juju list-controllers
Use --refresh flag with this command to see the latest information.

Controller          Model    User   Access     Cloud/Region   Models  Machines   HA    Version
my-aws-controller*  default  admin  superuser  aws/us-east-1     2         1     none  2.3.2
```

The preceding screenshot shows the AWS controller that we have deployed. In order to access the GUI type the following command:

```
juju gui
```

This command will give you the hyperlink and user credentials to log in to the GUI:

```
alokshrivastwa@instance-1:~$ juju gui
GUI 2.11.1 for model "admin/default" is enabled at:
  https://54.161.35.46:17070/gui/u/admin/default
Your login credential is:
  username: admin
  password: 6f4569afafd83bdf963e0b1dc994c266
alokshrivastwa@instance-1:~$
```

> The controller details you see in the previous image are for the purposes of this book, and the link will no longer be functional when you are reading it so will NOT work.

Also, remember that the SSL certificate will be self-signed, and therefore will not be trusted by your computer. Once we log in to the controller, we can start to model and deploy the applications.

Note that the details on modelling with Juju are beyond the scope of this book and hence will not be covered here:

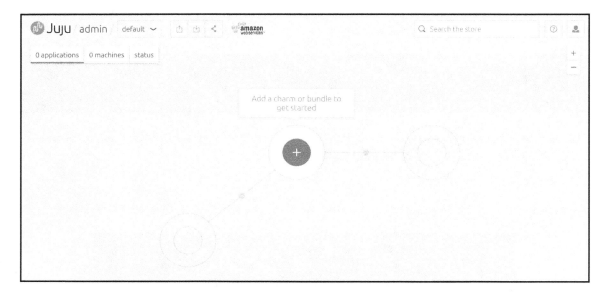

The dashboard provides several features of the Juju CLI.

Deploying Kubernetes with Juju

Now that we have our Juju functional, we can start to deploy a k8s cluster on it. The command in order to do so is as follows:

```
juju deploy canonical-kubernetes <other options>
```

The following screenshot shows the deployment of the Kubernetes cluster on the `default` controller, which in my case is the AWS controller:

```
alokshrivastwa@instance-1:~$ juju deploy canonical-kubernetes
Located bundle "cs:bundle/canonical-kubernetes-150"
Resolving charm: cs:~containers/easyrsa-27
Resolving charm: cs:~containers/etcd-63
Resolving charm: cs:~containers/flannel-40
Resolving charm: cs:~containers/kubeapi-load-balancer-43
Resolving charm: cs:~containers/kubernetes-master-78
Resolving charm: cs:~containers/kubernetes-worker-81
Executing changes:
- upload charm cs:~containers/easyrsa-27 for series xenial
- deploy application easyrsa on xenial using cs:~containers/easyrsa-27
  added resource easyrsa
- set annotations for easyrsa
- upload charm cs:~containers/etcd-63 for series xenial
- deploy application etcd on xenial using cs:~containers/etcd-63
  added resource etcd
  added resource snapshot
- set annotations for etcd
         .
         .
         .
         .
         .
- add unit easyrsa/0 to new machine 0
- add unit etcd/0 to new machine 1
- add unit etcd/1 to new machine 2
- add unit etcd/2 to new machine 3
- add unit kubeapi-load-balancer/0 to new machine 4
- add unit kubernetes-master/0 to new machine 5
- add unit kubernetes-worker/0 to new machine 6
- add unit kubernetes-worker/1 to new machine 7
- add unit kubernetes-worker/2 to new machine 8
Deploy of bundle completed.
alokshrivastwa@instance-1:~$
```

The preceding screenshot has been snipped to save space. Note that this bundle deploys a `production grade` Kubernetes cluster with nine nodes.

- One node: Easy RSA server for certificate management
- Three nodes: ETCD cluster for HA
- One node: Kubernetes master
- Three nodes: Kubernetes minions
- One node: Load balancer

Once the deployment is complete, you can see the connections on the Juju controller dashboard:

 Read more about this Juju bundle by visiting: `https://jujucharms.com/canonical-kubernetes/`

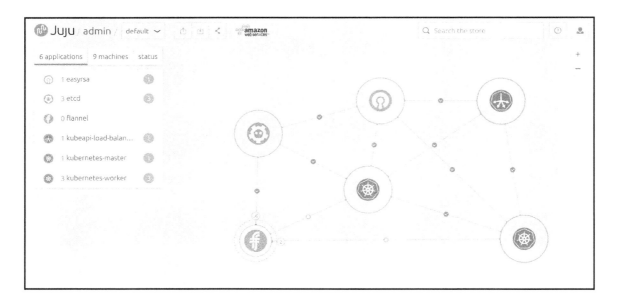

In order to see the machines and their IP addresses, execute the following command:

```
juju status
```

This will show the IP addresses and instance-ids of the server (please see the output snipped):

```
App                   Version  Status       Scale  Charm                 Store       Rev  OS      Notes
easyrsa               3.0.1    active           1  easyrsa               jujucharms    3  ubuntu
etcd                  3.1.2    active           3  etcd                  jujucharms   14  ubuntu
flannel               0.6.1    maintenance      4  flannel               jujucharms    5  ubuntu
kubeapi-load-balancer 1.10.0   active           1  kubeapi-load-balancer jujucharms    3  ubuntu  exposed
kubernetes-master     1.6.1    active           1  kubernetes-master     jujucharms    6  ubuntu
kubernetes-worker     1.6.1    active           3  kubernetes-worker     jujucharms    8  ubuntu  exposed
topbeat                        active           3  topbeat               jujucharms    5  ubuntu

Unit            Workload    Agent  Machine  Public address  Ports       Message
easyrsa/0*      active      idle   0        52.15.98.82                 Certificate Authority connected.
```

 Managing Kubernetes on AWS, you may choose to use projects such as HeptIO Authenticator `https://github.com/heptio/authenticator`, which allows us to use the AWS IAM with the Kubernetes directly.

Deploying a second instance of Kubernetes

Since we are making a hybrid cloud, we have to deploy a second instance of Kubernetes using Juju on the OpenStack environment.

In this case, the command is similar, however we need to mention the controller name and the model name of Juju. In our case, the controller name is OpenStack-RegionOne and the model name is default:

```
juju deploy canonical-kubernetes -m my-devstack-RegionOne:default
```

 To find data and model information about the controller, execute the `juju list-controllers` command.

Now, sit back and relax as the nodes get deployed to the private cloud environment. Execute the command, `juju status` with the `-m <controller name>:<model name>` flag to see the status:

```
juju status -m my-devstack-RegionOne:default
```

```
App                         Version  Status       Scale  Charm                   Store       Rev  OS      Notes
easyrsa                     3.0.1    maintenance      1  easyrsa                 jujucharms   27  ubuntu
etcd                                 waiting        2/3  etcd                    jujucharms   63  ubuntu
flannel                              waiting          0  flannel                 jujucharms   40  ubuntu
kubeapi-load-balancer                waiting        0/1  kubeapi-load-balancer   jujucharms   43  ubuntu  exposed
kubernetes-master                    waiting        0/1  kubernetes-master       jujucharms   78  ubuntu
kubernetes-worker                    waiting        0/3  kubernetes-worker       jujucharms   81  ubuntu  exposed

Unit                        Workload     Agent       Machine  Public address  Ports  Message
easyrsa/0*                  maintenance  executing   0        10.37.130.80           (install) installing charm software
etcd/0*                     maintenance  executing   1        10.37.130.149          (install) installing charm software
etcd/1                      maintenance  executing   2        10.37.130.75           (install) installing charm software
etcd/2                      waiting      allocating  3        10.37.130.102          waiting for machine
kubeapi-load-balancer/0     waiting      allocating  4        10.37.130.56           waiting for machine
kubernetes-master/0         waiting      allocating  5        10.37.130.19           waiting for machine
kubernetes-worker/0         waiting      allocating  6        10.37.130.99           waiting for machine
kubernetes-worker/1         waiting      allocating  7        10.37.130.57           waiting for machine
kubernetes-worker/2         waiting      allocating  8        10.37.130.220          waiting for machine

Machine  State    DNS            Inst id          Series  AZ  Message
0        started  10.37.130.80   juju-698e3a-0    xenial      Running
1        started  10.37.130.149  juju-698e3a-1    xenial      Running
2        started  10.37.130.75   juju-698e3a-2    xenial      Running
3        pending  10.37.130.102  juju-698e3a-3    xenial      Running
4        pending  10.37.130.56   juju-698e3a-4    xenial      Running
5        pending  10.37.130.19   juju-698e3a-5    xenial      Running
6        pending  10.37.130.99   juju-698e3a-6    xenial      Running
7        pending  10.37.130.57   juju-698e3a-7    xenial      Running
8        pending  10.37.130.220  juju-698e3a-8    xenial      Running

Relation provider                      Requirer                                 Interface         Type         Message
easyrsa:client                         etcd:certificates                        tls-certificates  regular      joining
easyrsa:client                         kubeapi-load-balancer:certificates       tls-certificates  regular      joining
easyrsa:client                         kubernetes-master:certificates           tls-certificates  regular      joining
easyrsa:client                         kubernetes-worker:certificates           tls-certificates  regular      joining
etcd:cluster                           etcd:cluster                             etcd              peer         joining
etcd:db                                flannel:etcd                             etcd              regular      joining
etcd:db                                kubernetes-master:etcd                   etcd              regular      joining
kubeapi-load-balancer:loadbalancer     kubernetes-master:loadbalancer           public-address    regular      joining
kubeapi-load-balancer:website          kubernetes-worker:kube-api-endpoint      http              regular      joining
kubernetes-master:cni                  flannel:cni                              kubernetes-cni    subordinate  joining
kubernetes-master:kube-api-endpoint    kubeapi-load-balancer:apiserver          http              regular      joining
kubernetes-master:kube-control         kubernetes-worker:kube-control           kube-control      regular      joining
kubernetes-worker:cni                  flannel:cni                              kubernetes-cni    subordinate  joining
```

It will take several minutes before the cluster turns active.

> If we are working on a certain controller, we may switch to it so the commands don't need to be appended with the `-m` flag.
>
> We can do so by using the command `juju switch <controller name>"`, this will make that controller the default.

Once ready, we can download the Kubernetes configuration file from the Kubernetes master and execute the commands.

Connecting to the Kubernetes clusters

Now that we have created the clusters using Juju, we need to copy the configuration file from the Kubernetes master. The configuration file can be copied over SCP.

I am going to copy these files to my Ubuntu server on which I have Juju installed. For this, I will create a directory called .kube (the preceding . will hide the folder).

```
juju switch aws
juju scp kubernetes-master/0:/home/ubuntu/config aws-config
mv aws-config .kube/

juju switch my-devstack
juju scp kubernetes-master/0:/home/ubuntu/config openstack-config
mv openstack-config .kube/
```

So, basically, I switched the Juju controllers, and from each of the Kubernetes masters that we had, we copied the file at the location /home/ubuntu/config.

Juju allows us to execute commands on the resources that it creates. For example, if we simply type the command juju ssh <resource name>, we will have logged into the resource from the Juju client. It is this feature of Juju that we have used to SCP the files to the client machine.

We copied both these files to our hidden kube directory. Next up, we have to install kubectl itself. Remember that kubectl is installed by default on the Kubernetes nodes, so, we can simply use the command there. However, please remember that the Ubuntu server (or your workstation) doesn't have kubectl, and therefore we have to install it.

In Ubuntu, we can simply install it by typing:

```
sudo snap install kubectl --classic
```

Please remember that the above command will only work if "snapd" is installed on Ubuntu. The "snaps" are universal linux packages working across several distributions of Linux.

Please refer to the https://docs.snapcraft.io/core/install in order to find the installation instructions for snapd itself on the linux distribution that you are using.

If the Operating System / Linux Distro doesn't support snap as per the previous link, we could install the kubectl binary using curl/wget. Please see the following link for steps to do so: `https://kubernetes.io/docs/tasks/tools/install-kubectl/#install-kubectl-binary-via-curl`

Once installed, kubectl needs its configuration file, named `config`, in the `.kube` directory, but since we have two of them we will pass them on the command line.

We will execute the `cluster-info` command to see the Kubernetes cluster:

```
alokshrivastwa@instance-1:~$ kubectl cluster-info --kubeconfig=.kube/openstack-config
Kubernetes master is running at https://10.37.130.56:443
Heapster is running at https://10.37.130.56:443/api/v1/namespaces/kube-system/services/heapster/proxy
KubeDNS is running at https://10.37.130.56:443/api/v1/namespaces/kube-system/services/kube-dns:dns/proxy
kubernetes-dashboard is running at https://10.37.130.56:443/api/v1/namespaces/kube-system/services/https:kubernetes-dashboard:/proxy
Grafana is running at https://10.37.130.56:443/api/v1/namespaces/kube-system/services/monitoring-grafana/proxy
InfluxDB is running at https://10.37.130.56:443/api/v1/namespaces/kube-system/services/monitoring-influxdb:http/proxy
```

As we can see, the Kubernetes cluster is running. We can now execute the Kubernetes commands on this cluster.

Federation using Kubernetes

We finally come to the section of the book that we have been waiting for, that is, to make these two isolated Kubernetes clusters communicate and work with each other. This is done using a feature called the **KubeFed**.

The following link talks about cluster federation in detail: `https://kubernetes.io/docs/tasks/federation/set-up-cluster-federation-kubefed/`

At the time of writing, Kubefed is *beta* and is only used by companies that are running cutting edge technology. In this, we create a new Kubernetes cluster, which is specifically used to federate the other Kubernetes clusters and not host the pods themselves.

The *Federated* service (the **service** in the federated cluster) is much like a normal k8s service but it performs the following functions:

- Deploys the same Kubernetes services in every underlying cluster that is joined to the cluster federation.
- Monitors the health of those services.
- Manages DNS records in a public DNS provider (such as Google Cloud DNS, AWS Route 53, and so on), to help find the closest service in the same cluster or the nearest cluster.

Clients inside your federated Kubernetes clusters (that is, pods) will automatically find the local shard of the federated service in their cluster if it exists and is healthy, or the closest healthy shard in a different cluster.

The following diagram will help us understand the federation concept:

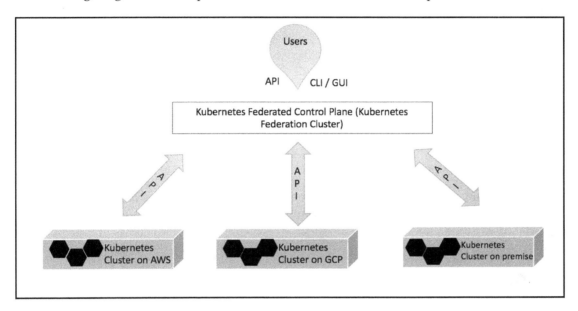

The users talk to the federation cluster and not to the actual Kubernetes cluster, and the federation enables us to have a cluster of clusters. Please note, that the networking (container networking such as Flannel) needs to be configured for it to work and the federation cluster will manage the DNS for us.

Reasons for consideration

Now, that we know what Kubernetes is and what a federation of the Kubernetes clusters would look like, the real question from an architectural perspective is, why should we even consider it?

The following section will try and answer that question for us.

Application migration – avoiding vendor lock-in

Having a federated cluster will allow us to seamlessly migrate applications from one infrastructure provider/data center to the other with minimal effort. If designed for it (using global databases) we can do this in near real-time. It would also make the whole migration scriptable, which means we can schedule it and trigger it.

There are several indications that once cloud service innovation plateaus, it will become a utility provider - along the same lines as electricity and water. It will become standardized, and possibly even traded, like the current stock market.

This means there might be a reason to be on cloud provider A on day 1, and on cloud provider B on day 2, and then back to cloud provider A on day 3. Having a federated Kubernetes cluster will definitely help in achieving that dream.

The ability to move between infrastructure providers will also help us avoid vendor lock-in, and hence will allow the enterprises to regain some degree of control in the event of cost / support negotiations with the infrastructure providers.

Enforce policies

Having a federated Kubernetes cluster will also allow us to enforce policies across the infrastructure providers. Kubernetes allows network and security policies to be applied across clusters.

A sample of a restrictive security policy sample has been shown—refer to the link `https://kubernetes.io/docs/concepts/policy/pod-security-policy/` for the pod security policy. While pod security policy is beyond the scope of this book, let us take a look at its core constructs.

We start with the version and the kind of security policy. In the restricted example that is being referred to, the version is version 1, beta 1 (`v1beta1`). This is important, because depending on the version that is specified, the different keys in the file will be comprehended.

```
apiVersion: extensions/v1beta1
kind: PodSecurityPolicy
```

In the next section of the policy, we provide the metadata for the security policy. In the example, we are specifying a name for the security policy, and also the annotations, which are used to specify specific App Armor and Sec Comp profiles to be used by the containers.

```
metadata:
  name: restricted
  annotations:
    seccomp.security.alpha.kubernetes.io/allowedProfileNames:  'docker/default'
    apparmor.security.beta.kubernetes.io/allowedProfileNames:  'runtime/default'
    seccomp.security.alpha.kubernetes.io/defaultProfileName:   'docker/default'
    apparmor.security.beta.kubernetes.io/defaultProfileName:   'runtime/default'
```

The next section of the policy has the specifications that need to be met in order for the pod to be provisioned. This section has several controls as we can see in the example policy.

```
spec:
  privileged: false
  allowPrivilegeEscalation: false
  requiredDropCapabilities:
    - ALL
  volumes:
    - 'configMap'
    - 'emptyDir'
    - 'projected'
    - 'secret'
    - 'downwardAPI'
    - 'persistentVolumeClaim'
  hostNetwork: false
  hostIPC: false
  hostPID: false
  runAsUser:
    rule: 'MustRunAsNonRoot'
  seLinux:
    rule: 'RunAsAny'
  supplementalGroups:
    rule: 'MustRunAs'
    ranges:
      - min: 1
        max: 65535
  fsGroup:
    rule: 'MustRunAs'
    ranges:
      - min: 1
        max: 65535
  readOnlyRootFilesystem: false
```

As we can see from the file:

- We have disallowed the system to run as `root` and also disabled privilege escalation (using `privileged`, `allowPrivilegeEscalation`, and `runAsUser`)
- We have allowed it to run as `group-id` from `1` through `65535`, which is a general purpose user—remember that UID of the root is `0`
- We have allowed all kinds of volumes to be attached to the system, using the `volumes` switch
- We have *not* allowed it to share the HostPID namespace (of the container) with the host – `hostPID` switch
- We have also disallowed the container from sharing the network and IPC namespace with the host – `hostNetwork` and `hostIPC` switch

There are other settings that can be specified, such as what paths from the host can be referenced by containers and so on. This allows there to be restrictions in the communication ability of different containers. Due to these abilities, this also helps us enforce compliance and regulatory policies, such as on-premises and air-gapping applications, environments, and so on.

High availability and application upgrades

The federation allows for high availability of applications, as the controllers (Replication Controllers and Deployment Controllers) can bring a complete application up in event of a failure in a cloud. This allows us to be immune to any unavoidable outages of the cloud providers.

This also allows us to upgrade the applications (Canary Upgrades), which is a feature of Kubernetes, and apply it over multiple public cloud providers.

Cloud bursting

This is the most important Hybrid Cloud use case, where we can use a public cloud to augment the capacity in the private cloud/private data center. Kubernetes federation allows us to do that. It also helps and assists us to make choices based on availability and cost requirements of the applications.

Federation challenges

The architecture decision will not be considered complete if we don't consider the challenges posed by the federation:

- **Public cloud data-transfer costs**: I often *jokingly* say that the cloud needs something from us, either data, or money. Most public cloud providers allow free upload to the cloud (they are getting our data) and they charge if the data is moved out of it - which we do when we download the data. In a cross cloud cluster, there will be data transfer charges as we will be moving the data between two infrastructure providers.
- **Reliability and latency considerations**: We all know that a chain is only as strong as its weakest link, and in any application, when it is being passed around, the weakest reliability of the link becomes the overall reliability of the system. It's the same calculation that we do for SLA. Say there are two parties each providing 99% uptime for their individual pieces. Then the application's availability will become 98% (99% * 99% (that is, - 0.99 * 0.99) = 0.9801 = 98.01%). So the greater the number of components there are, the lesser the reliability.
- **Monitoring consolidations**: This is a major one for the hybrid cloud scenario. Since different clouds provide different methods of monitoring and even different metrics, we need a way to consolidate them to effectively operationalize a hybrid cloud.

Implementing a Kubernetes federation

The federation of a Kubernetes cluster is implemented using the kubefed system. The official documentation for federation is available at: `https://kubernetes.io/docs/tasks/federation/set-up-cluster-federation-kubefed/`.

The requirements of implementing a Kubernetes federation is fairly straightforward:

- A DNS provider that can be manipulated with AP's - Currently, Google Cloud Platform and AWS Route 53 are supported. If there is none, we can use the `etcd` in the federation controller in order to host the DNS. We will then need to use the proper NS records to redirect to the DNS server.
- Another Kubernetes cluster where kubefed will be installed.

We will use Juju to set up the clusters.

> Remember, we can use the two clusters that we created earlier in the chapter, we simply have to create another one where the federation needs to be enabled.
>
> We can create the federation cluster either on another project in OpenStack, or we can deploy it on another AWS region. The idea will be to bootstrap another Juju controller.

Step 1 – setting up the federation controller

This is similar to how we set the other controllers. In this case, we will bootstrap it on to the local LxD controller. However, you can bootstrap it on to another region in the AWS. Optionally, a new model can be added to the existing controller. In our case, we will do the same rather than creating a new controller.

> A Juju controller can host multiple models for different types of workloads. Say for instance, we have to deploy four different instances of MySQL, we will need four different models for it, as a single charm can only be deployed once per model per controller.

We will use the `juju add-model` command to create a new model in the exiting controller.

```
juju add-model federation-kubernetes
```

The preceding command will create a new model and switch to it. In order to list all the models, execute the command `juju models`:

> In order to switch to a different controller/model pair, use the command,
> `juju switch <controller name>:<model name>`

We will deploy Kubernetes using the same command as we did earlier:

```
juju deploy canonical-kubernetes
```

Wait for some time for it to deploy the nine-machine cluster. Monitor the status using the `juju status` command. Once the third Kubernetes cluster is set up we will download the configuration file for the third cluster as well. The same commands as before will be used:

```
juju scp kubernetes-master/0:/home/ubuntu/config config
mv config .kube/
```

The preceding command will make this the default configuration of the Kubectl command.

Step 2 – combining the Kubernetes configuration (optional)

Working on the Kubernetes cluster will now become cumbersome, as we will then have to switch the configuration files every time we operate on the different clusters. There is a script that can combine the different Kubernetes configurations into a single file, which we can switch with the `--context` switch.

The `load-kubeconfig` tool is available at `https://github.com/Collaborne/load-kubeconfig`. The tool can be installed with the following command:

```
sudo npm install -g load-kubeconfig
```

Once installed, we will then add the two configurations that we procured earlier. We will first change the names of the context in the files before we can load it. In the following example, we replace the words `juju-context` and `juju-cluster` with AWS in the file `aws-config`. While we can do this manually, the following `sed` command will help us achieve it:

```
sed -i -e "s/juju-cluster/aws/g" \
    -e "s/juju-context/aws/g" \
    .kube/aws-config
```

We will repeat the same for the `openstack-config` and the `config` (from the federation cluster) file as well. The command will be shown as follows:

```
sed -i -e "s/juju-cluster/openstack/g" \
    -e "s/juju-context/openstack/g" \
    .kube/openstack-config

sed -i -e "s/juju-cluster/fed-cluster/g" \
    -e "s/juju-context/fed-cluster/g" \
    .kube/config
```

The file will look like this after the modification (the replaced values are highlighted):

```
alokshrivastwa@instance-1:~$ sed -i -e "s/juju-cluster/openstack/g" \
>    -e "s/juju-context/openstack/g" \
>    .kube/openstack-config
alokshrivastwa@instance-1:~$
alokshrivastwa@instance-1:~$
alokshrivastwa@instance-1:~$ cat .kube/openstack-config
apiVersion: v1
clusters:
- cluster:



    server: https://10.37.130.56:443
  name: openstack
contexts:
- context:
    cluster: openstack
    user: admin
  name: openstack
current-context: openstack
kind: Config
preferences: {}
users:
- name: admin
  user:
    as-user-extra: {}
    password: iwuSjPDh1lVoQPnSuGbMhnLM9dMJplyc
    username: admin
alokshrivastwa@instance-1:~$
```

Once complete, execute the following commands to merge the config files:

```
load-kubeconfig .kube/aws-config
load-kubeconfig .kube/openstack-config
```

This will merge the configuration with the `.kube/config` file (please remember that the base file was from the federation controller that we just downloaded). We can henceforth use the command using the `--context` switch and pass the names we just substituted, that is, aws, openstack, and fed-cluster.

We can check the contexts that are available for us to use by using the following command:

```
kubectl config get-contexts
```

Step 3 – creating the federation

Now we are ready to create the federation. In this, we have to first configure the DNS service provider. Since we are going to use a cloud agnostic DNS provider, we will use the Core DNS provider.

Creating the DNS provider

We will first switch to the federation cluster and enable the core DNS system:

```
juju switch federation-kubernetes
juju config kubernetes-master enable-coredns=True
```

We will then find the IP of the machine with the etcd cluster using the juju status command. We will create a file called dns-config.conf with the following content:

```
[Global]
etcd-endpoints = http://<IP of etcd cluster>:2379
zones = federation-test.com
```

Initializing the federation

We will initialize the federation with the DNS configuration. We will need to install the kubefed tool in order to manage the federation of the cluster. It is installed with the same snap plugin we used earlier in the chapter:

```
sudo snap install kubefed --classic
```

Once the install is complete, we can use it to configure the federation using the kubefed init command. We will pass a few parameters:

```
kubefed init federation --host-cluster-context=fed-cluster --dns-
provider="coredns" --dns-zone-name="federation-test.com." --dns-provider-
config=dns-config.conf
```

Once the cluster is ready, we can then start to add the clusters to the federation:

```
kubectl config use-context federation
kubefed join openstack --host-cluster-context=fed-cluster
kubefed join aws --host-cluster-context=fed-cluster
```

This will add the clusters to our federation. Congratulations, we are ready. Now, we can create pods and they will go to both the clusters, depending on the affinity and anti-affinity rules.

Summary

Now we have seen the architecture and the deployment models for Kubernetes-based hybrid clouds. Please note that it is still in pre-release at the time of writing this book. This method of building a hybrid cloud gives us the most advantages in this scenario.

Kubefed is still in beta, is mainly tested on the GKE, and is one of the best choices for use in production right now. The main points to keep in mind while designing a federated cluster are: the state of all applications resides in the actual cluster, the federation supports about 100 clusters, and each cluster supports approximately 10000 nodes.

Clusters can fail independently of each other, so failures are easy to manage. In the next few chapters, we will deal with operating the hybrid cloud and some of the concepts involved in this.

8
Using PreBuilt Hybrid Cloud Solutions

In the last few chapters, we have seen how to build a hybrid cloud with a CMP, as well as a containerized version. However, in order to make it easier for us to adopt the hybrid cloud, some companies have created a hybrid cloud solution. In this chapter, we will look at the different options that we have and weigh our options.

Here, we are going to take a look at the following main options:

- Azure Stack
- OpenStack Omni
- vCloud Air

There are some other players in the market, but these three will be enough to give us an idea of the details of these kinds of systems.

Azure Stack

Azure Stack was launched by Microsoft in 2016 to fill the void of the *hybrid cloud*. It was for organizations that couldn't, or wouldn't, move to the public cloud due to compliance or regulatory requirements.

In the most simple terms, it provides an Azure-like experience on your personal hardware in your private data center / Co-Lo (Colocation) data center.

Azure Stack provides only a subset of services provided by Azure.

The following table shows the services that are provided by the Azure Stack:

Category	Services offered (Azure terminology)
Compute	Virtual Machines, Service Fabric
Data Storage	Blobs, Tables, Queues
Network	Virtual Network, LoadBalancer, VPN Gateway
Management & Security	Azure Portal, KeyVault
Developer Services	Azure SDK
Web & Mobile	Logic Apps, Web Apps, Mobile Apps, API Apps

If you notice, the list is mainly about IaaS services of the Azure platform (with some PaaS). The cognitive services are not present and this is for a good reason, because they will require large amounts of computation power (in the background), which cannot be assumed in a private environment.

Getting the Azure Stack

Azure Stack is general available. In order to run Azure Stack however, we will need some integrated hardware from the pre-approved vendors. At this moment, only HP, Dell, and Lenovo have been approved at the time of writing this book, however, Cisco, Avanade, and others will join in soon.

See the following for the recommended hardware specifications. You should be aware that we wouldn't be able to run it on a laptop: `https://docs.microsoft.com/en-us/azure/azure-stack/azure-stack-deploy`.

According to the recommended settings, we will need a server with:

- One OS disk 200 GB
- Four disks (140 GB - minimum, 250 GB - recommended)
- CPU (dual socket - 12 cores - minimum, 16 cores - recommended)
- Memory (96 GB minimum, 128 GB recommended)

The installation of a single node POC is shown in the following video: `https://channel9.msdn.com/Blogs/azurestack/Microsoft-Azure-Stack-TP1-POC-Deployment-Tutorial`.

In essence, we download and unzip the Azure Stack files, and install it once the base requirements, such as enabling RDP, cookies, and so on, are done.

Azure Stack can be purchased in two versions:

- Self managed
- Managed service

In the former, we have to purchase the hardware from the supported vendors and the software from Microsoft. The system is traditionally run in the private data center.

The **managed service** on the other hand would be more of a co-location arrangement with a supported vendor.

Azure Stack runs a bunch of Microsoft products such as Hyper-V, SQL, and so on. Hence, we need to worry about the licensing too. Azure Stack also comes in two plans, the *pay-as-you-go* model and the *Capacity* model. It is covered in a little more detail in the next section.

Both models are licensed through the **Enterprise Agreement** (**EA**), and pay-as-you-go can be licensed through a **Cloud Service Provider** (**CSP**) as well.

If the system is always connected to Azure, then the pay-as-you-go model is applicable for the licenses (that it takes to run the Azure Stack). However, if this is not possible, then the capacity model license can be procured based on the number of physical cores on the system.

Refer to the following link for pricing and licensing details:

`https://azure.microsoft.com/en-in/overview/azure-stack/how-to-buy/`

 The detailed architecture of the Azure Stack is beyond the purview of the book, however Packt Publishing have a detailed book titled **Building Hybrid Cloud with Azure Stack** with ISBN 978-1786466297.

OpenStack Omni

The next major contender in the space is OpenStack. Now, OpenStack is the most highly adopted service down cloud, and powers several public and private clouds out there, so it is only natural that this becomes a candidate for the hybrid cloud.

While OpenStack, by default, includes the required systems to create an OpenStack-only hybrid cloud (the private cloud can simply be added as a new region in the Horizon dashboard), it still doesn't work with other clouds.

So, if we were to have our private cloud based on OpenStack, and the public based on AWS, this would not have been possible without a third-party CMP (as we saw in `Chapter 6`, *Building a Traditional CMP-Based Hybrid Cloud*). In order to bridge this gap, Platform9 (`http://www.platform9.com`) has created a new project under the OpenStack "big-tent" governance model (`https://www.openstack.org/videos/vancouver-2015/the-big-tent-a-look-at-the-new-openstack-projects-governance`) called **Omni**.

 At the time of writing the book, the Big Tent model of OpenStack governance is being reconsidered in the facor of a "modular" governance model and hence the Big Tent services may change soon.

OpenStack Omni allows the integration between OpenStack environments and AWS. This again works like any other, where the project extends OpenStack to be able to request and manage the resources from the AWS environments.

 At the time of writing this book, the Omni drivers were available for AWS and GCP, and still under development for Microsoft Azure.

The concepts are similar to that of the CMP, where the credentials are added and the Omni system makes the required API calls. Please do note, that these also work mainly with IaaS services.

Installing OpenStack Omni on DevStack

Omni is being developed as a community effort, so the way we run this project is by installing it from the source on GitHub (`https://github.com/openstack/omni`). However, for the purposes of this book, we can simply add this to our `devstack` environment that we created.

The installation of Omni includes modifications to Nova, Neutron, Cinder, and Glance, in addition to the Horizon dashboard. The API keys and new drivers are injected into the systems to make OpenStack work with AWS and GCP.

However, using it in `devstack` simply means enabling the `omni` plugin, and setting the configuration variables in the familiar `local.conf` file that we used to set the `devstack` up (refer to earlier chapters).

The steps are the following:

1. Remove the `devstack` instance that is running—it will remove any virtual machines that were created and were running.
2. Modify the `local.conf` file.
3. Run `devstack`.

 At the time of writing, there were some bugs in the script that did not allow the `devstack` instance to come up properly. We shall discuss them and the way to fix them along the way, we have also requested the fixes to be merged upstream, so by the time you are reading the book, those extra changes need not be required.

Removing the DevStack instance

You need to SSH to the server where the `devstack` is running, just change the directory to `/devstack/` (if you followed along with this book) and execute the command `./unstack.sh`:

```
alokshrivastwa@instance-1:~$ sudo su
root@instance-1:/home/alokshrivastwa# su stack
stack@instance-1:/home$ cd /devstack/
stack@instance-1:/devstack$ ./unstack.sh
```

This will run the unstacking script and DevStack is removed from the system. Another simple way would have been to reboot the server. However, this is **not recommended** as it may not be a clean shutdown of DevStack, and restacking may pose a few issues.

Modifying the local.conf file

Edit the `local.conf` file located at `/devstack/local.conf` (if you have followed the book), we will add the `omni` plugin to this:

```
enable_plugin omni https://github.com/openstack/omni.git
```

Once this has been done, we will also use the plugin to configure the different services. In this example, we will set the `omni` to configure itself as AWS and hence, we need to pass the AWS access key and secret key. We can also pass the region and AZ name (as described on the Git page of Omni):

```
OMNI_PROVIDER=aws
SECRET_KEY=<Enter your Secret Key>
ACCESS_KEY=<Enter your Access Key>
```

Once you modify the file, the file should look something like this:

```
alokshrivastwa@instance-1:~$ cat /devstack/local.conf | grep -v "#" | grep -v ^$
[[local|localrc]]
ADMIN_PASSWORD=pass4adminUser
DATABASE_PASSWORD=stackdb
RABBIT_PASSWORD=stackqueue
SERVICE_PASSWORD=$ADMIN_PASSWORD
ENABLED_SERVICES+=,heat,h-eng,h-api,h-api-cfn,h-api-cw
enable_plugin omni https://github.com/openstack/omni.git
OMNI_PROVIDER=aws
SECRET_KEY=
ACCESS_KEY=
LOGFILE=$DEST/logs/stack.sh.log
LOGDAYS=2
SWIFT_HASH=66a3d6b56c1f479c8b4e70ab5c2000f5
SWIFT_REPLICAS=1
SWIFT_DATA_DIR=$DEST/data
alokshrivastwa@instance-1:~$
```

Running DevStack

DevStack can now be launched with the command, `/devstack/stack.sh`. This will run the system with Omni.

See the video from Platform9 about the operation of the Omni project at: `https://www.youtube.com/watch?v=cceXCjnP-LU`.

The OpenStack system will now be communicating with the AWS environment. In order to modify the keys, we have to modify it in the configuration files of Nova, Cinder, Glance, and Neutron, and then restart the services.

At the time of writing this book, OpenStack Omni's maturity was still not suitable for use in production, however this may change in the future depending upon the requirements of the industry.

vCloud Air

vCloud Air was launched by VMware in early 2013, but now is a part of a French cloud service provider, OVH. Basically **vCloud air** is the public cloud built atop of VMware technologies such as vSphere and vRA - the vRealize Automation suite of products, which is the infrastructure down CMP offering from VMware itself.

The system added the public cloud counterpart onto a vRealize-based private cloud setup. Since the underlying technology will be VMware in both places, it will make it easier to move the machines around and use the same templates, thereby making it hybrid.

In order to get more details about the service offering, navigate to: `https:/ /www.vmware.com/in/cloud-services/infrastructure.html`

vCloud Air provides services for:

- Disaster recovery
- Data center extension
- Data center replacement

The services are predominantly IaaS, and services are backed by VMware technologies such as VMware SRM, VMware vSphere, VMware ESXi, and so on.

Using the different hybrid cloud solutions

As we have seen some pre-built hybrid cloud solutions, we have surely understood that this is an extension of having a CMP for the hybrid cloud. However, in this case, the CMP is either pre-built and pre-configured (sometimes even managed), so the functionality is not very different.

Having seen the different options that are available for us in order to create a hybrid cloud, let's take a look at some of the architectural patterns that we will use to decide which solution is the best for us.

Lets enumerate the options we have:

1. CMP-based - DIY—*Do It Yourself* (`Chapter 6`, *Building a Traditional CMP-Based Hybrid Cloud*)
2. Containers-based - DIY—*Do It Yourself* (`Chapter 7`, *Building a Containerized Hybrid Cloud*)
3. CMP-based—pre-built (current chapter)

Let's divide them into two—CMP-based and container-based:

Feature	CMP-based	Container orchestration-based
Field of action	IaaS, PaaS (limited)	PaaS, DevOps
Focus	Control	Speed
Use cases	Traditional applications - monolithic, n-tier, and so on	Microservices-oriented (while one may run a monolith inside a container, that's not the most optimal use)
Cost	FOSS too expensive	FOSS too expensive
Use it for	Enabling self-service, implementing common automation.	Eliminating/automating infrastructure plumbing, DevOps
Learning curve	Low to medium	High to very high

So, in most traditional enterprises, a CMP-based system should be more than sufficient. However, in modern enterprises, trying to move toward a microservice architecture and enabling cloud bursting will definitely mean using container orchestration platforms.

Another consideration is that pre-built solutions are a little expensive. However, they simplify the process of deployment and are easier in this respect.

Summary

In summary, we have seen that the pre-built solutions mainly follow the CMP model of a hybrid cloud, and they may help us build a hybrid cloud faster and operate it better. However, the solution is not without lock-in.

It may be prudent for one to use a pre-built solution if we need to transfer the risk to the vendor, rather than keeping it with us. The downside is that we are stuck with the features that the solution provides. This may not be a downside for most organizations, but it will certainly hurt organizations with bleeding edge technology.

In the upcoming chapters, we deal with operating the hybrid clouds that we have built, as well as the different tools that are available for service down clouds and how they might apply to a use case.

9
DevOps in the Hybrid Cloud

One of the most important changes that the enterprises need to go through is the tooling needed for operationalizing the cloud. While most of the traditional tools work in *infrastructure up* clouds, in the service down clouds, there is some additional tooling that we can use in order to make it even easier.

In this chapter, we will deal with the tooling that is available in order for us to be able to make a DevOps **Continuous Integration/Continuous Deployment (CI/CD)** toolchain. There are several tools that the public cloud itself provides; however, we will need to use a common tooling when we are dealing with a hybrid cloud.

The development cycle and DevOps

When creating an application, companies follow either a waterfall model or an agile methodology of project management. While there are several changes in how things are done in both of the methods, technically, the steps followed are not that different.

Each software development cycle technically consists of:

- Requirement gathering (for bugs or new features)
- Development/coding
- Integration of code
- Testing the code
- Deployment

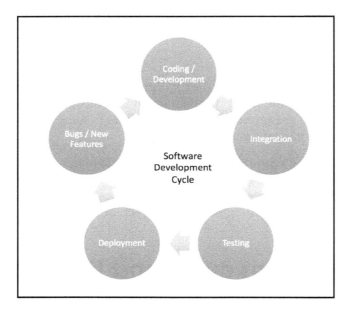

It is a cyclic process and continuously improves the software that is being written. The waterfall and agile have different philosophies of how to perform these steps; the steps themselves don't change.

For example, the agile development works on the whole cycle in *sprints*, which are normally two weeks to four weeks long as opposed to a long development cycle in that of a waterfall model.

Now assume we have to code, integrate, test, and deploy a specific feature within this short time, we will definitely need automation and tooling. Hence, it becomes even more relevant in the new coding practices.

Gartner introduced the Bimodal IT concept and coined two terms called **mode-1** and **mode-2** of the development. While mode-1's philosophy was very close to that of a traditional *waterfall model* development, the mode-2 is akin to *agile*, with one major difference. We can create any software in the agile methodology, but mode-2 is used for the software that is being created without all the answers known, which means a sprint can be used in order to change the product strategy and/or roadmap.

Refer to the following link for more information: `https://www.gartner.com/it-glossary/bimodal/`.

The traditional development stages

In the traditional software development process, a typical software goes through the following stages—this is not an exhaustive list but all the major milestones are mentioned. Note that some organizations tend to add or remove their own stages.

The knowledge of the following should help us understand the advent of cloud and also the tooling that we will talk about in the remainder of the chapter:

Stage	Description	Team/person responsible
Requirement gathering	In this the requirement of the software that is being created is gotten and documented.	Development team—product lead
Architecture	Here, the product architecture is made and the code practices that are to be followed are defined. This also takes into account the code deployment architecture—the number of machines that will be required to run the software, and so on.	Development team—application architect
Division of work	Here the code base to be written is divided into modules and assigned to different teams/set of people for parallelizing and development.	Development team—application architect/module leaders
Requisition of development and testing environment	The team then makes a request for the development environment. This is the most stripped-down version of what the production would look like.	Development team—project manager

Requisition of UAT and production environments	The team also makes a request for a testing environment and **user acceptance test** (**UAT**) environment. The UAT environment is created close (in specifications) to the production environment.	Development team—project manager
Provisioning infrastructure	The operations team provision the resources for the different environments that were requested. They perform functions such as creating the virtual/physical machines, assigning networks, creating DNS records, and assigning load balancers.	Operations team—network team and server team
Provisioning the platform	The platform team then installs and configures the middleware and the platforms that are needed for the different environments. For example, installing and initializing the database (MySQL, Oracle, MS SQL, Cassandra, MongoDB, and so on), application server (Tomcat/JBoss), and web server (Apache/IIS) atop the machines given by the infrastructure team.	Operations team—platform team
Development	This implies actual coding of the software modules.	Development team—developer
Unit testing	This is done to test each unit (for example: class, interface, function) of the software that is written and normally developed by the developer and module as a whole.	Development team—developer
Integration	This is an activity when the different modules that are developed independently are integrated with each other.	Development team—developer
Integration testing	This is a test that is performed to check whether the modules work well together, and also that they don't break each other. This is performed on the testing environment.	Development team—testing team
Deploy to UAT environment	The deployment to the UAT environment for the code is done.	Operations team—server team

UAT	The UAT is performed to check the functioning of all the components together; the performance of the software, the user experience and so on, are all tested here.	Development team—testing team/users
Deploy to production/cutover	The deployment of the code is done to the production environment and depending on the methodology—blue/green deployment or canary deployment—the cutover is done.	Operations team—server team

As we can see that two disparate teams (and their subteams) with very different skill sets are involved in making the application a reality. As we have seen this in the preceding section, there are several hand-offs between them.

If we were to enumerate the skills and functions between the teams, it will be presented as shown in the following diagram:

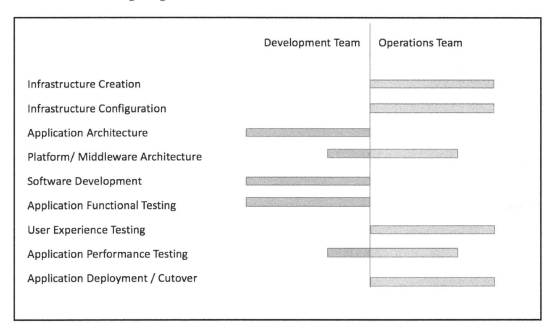

As we can see that there are very few places where they work together (for example, performance testing), but in most cases, it's a hand off.

The phenomenon of shuttling between the teams is most times referred to as **throwing code over the wall**, since most of the time there is very little communication between the teams.

The loss/miscommunication during the hand off and the time taken to shuttle between the two teams increases the time taken to get the software out of the door, thereby increasing the time to market.

Merging the different teams

We have seen the process and the problems in the previous sections, so what can be the theoretically straightforward solution? Merge both the teams!

However, the skills of the teams are fairly varied. For example, a development team is more focused on a language in which they are developing the software (for example, C#, Python, Java, and so on) and their expertise lies in this domain.

The operations team on the other hand are concerned with products and since they support multiple development teams, their expertise is on several platforms and products, most times from various vendors, as an example, operating systems such as Linux, Windows, and Unix; web servers such as Apache and IIS; database servers such as MySQL, MS SQL, and Oracle; networks such as Cisco and Juniper.

So, naturally, the problem is breadth, with multiple systems, versus depth in a single language to be able to code; hence, merging them was not very straightforward, but seemed to be the only way.

Now, thinking of the solution, our options are as follows:

- To train the development team about infrastructure operations
- To train the operations team about development
- To create a common team with members from both the teams

Now, we can also assume that maybe we may have to use more than one of the earlier mentioned options.

Thinking about it a little more, we can arrive at the conclusion that it will be easier to transition the responsibility of the operations team. So, if we can *codify* the function of the operations, it can be essentially categorized in three ways:

- Create the infrastructure (creation of a different environment)
- Configure the infrastructure (configuration of a different environment)
- Templatize (deployment of code in a different environment)

Creating the infrastructure

Since the introduction of virtualization, the infrastructure is becoming more software defined and thereby helping our cause; however, still some product-centric features seep in.

In order to bridge the gap, the service down philosophy was formed. The philosophy not only treated the infrastructure as fungible, which can be replaced with anything equivalent, but also broke the infrastructure down as simplified *lego-blocks*, which can be provisioned using API calls and can be used interchangeably.

This way, the developers don't have to bother with the nuances of each of the products and the service down platform will take care of them. Now, developers could request their own infrastructure without being bothered as to which vendors' hardware it was running on, which virtualization layer is used, which storage vendors' solution is used, and so on.

As this was focused toward the developer, the infrastructure was treated as *code* and hence the terminology **Infrastructure as a Code (IaaC)** or sometimes simply **IaC** was conceived and implemented.

 The IaaC is a distinguishing feature of a service down cloud. AWS has CloudFormation, OpenStack has Heat, Azure has Azure Resource Manager Templates, and Google has its Cloud Deployment Manager.

This allows us to create the infrastructures, version them, roll them back, and treat them as we would with any other software. A sample of the Amazon CloudFormation template can be found at `https://docs.aws.amazon.com/AWSCloudFormation/latest/UserGuide/sample-templates-services-us-west-2.html`.

While each of the clouds have their own IaC, we are introducing HashiCorp's **Terraform** (`https://www.terraform.io`), which is a multicloud IaC system that can work alongside multiple cloud providers and even custom cloud platforms.

Configuring the infrastructure

The second most important aspect is configuration of the infrastructure. The configuration of the infrastructure doesn't just mean the original configuration, but also deployment of the software that is written, perform canary upgrades, blue-green deployments, and so on.

Configuration management systems help us in managing the configuration of the infrastructure. There are several systems, which allow us to manage the configuration of the servers and several of them are open source.

The distinction in the configuration management systems are as follows:

- Agent based, for example, Chef and Puppet
- Agentless, for example, Ansible

These systems have the ability to abstract the actual commands required for configuring the system and instead use a common language across all the different operating systems.

 Please do remember that different configuration management systems use different languages, for example, Chef uses Ruby, Puppet uses its own language called DSL, based on Ruby, and so on.

As a sample of common use of language to configure multiple operating systems, see the following screenshot of a Chef recipe, where the recipe would install the Apache package:

```
package 'Install Apache' do
  case node[:platform]
  when 'redhat', 'centos'
    package_name 'httpd'
  when 'ubuntu', 'debian'
    package_name 'apache2'
  end
end
```

If we look closely, the Chef recipe checks the platform where it is running, and changes the package name. In the previous example, it would install HTTPD on RHEL and CentOS and the package is called `apache2` in the Debian-based Linux distributions.

Now, assume that we had to do this without using a configuration management software, we have to take care of the following two things:

1. Write a shell script in order to install the software; a sample shell script to install Apache (do the exact same thing as the preceding Chef recipe, shown as follows).
2. Create a delivery and execution mechanism—we could do it by hand, or write another bootstrap script in order to copy this file to a remote server and execute it using SSH, and so on:

```bash
#!/bin/bash
# Script to install Apache on multiple Linux Distros
# Author : Alok A S
# Version : 0.1

## Algorithm: Find the platform and install the appropriate
package
## We can do that by the lsb_release -a command or by the
looking at the *release files in the /etc location
## If Debian based system, then we will use the apt-get
command, else the yum package manager

cat /etc/*-release | grep -i debian
if [ $? -eq 0 ]; then
  echo "Debian Distro Found"
  sudo apt-get install -y apache2
  exit
fi

cat /etc/*-release | grep -i redhat
if [ $? -eq 0 ]; then
  echo "Redhat Distro Found"
  sudo yum install -y httpd
  exit
fi
```

As you can see that the complete onus is on us, and this increases the chances of us making mistakes.

Other than simplifying the scripting and the delivery of the scripts that are required in order to install and configure the system, the configuration management systems also allow the different parts of the install to share information with each other, create dependencies, which means multiple scripts can be logically stringed together to execute and perform complicated functions.

Configuration management systems also perform functions such as writing configuration files, copying files, and executing shell scripts. So the use of a configuration management system becomes absolutely a no-brainer regardless of whether we use a service down cloud or not.

Templatize

The final piece of the puzzle is deploying the software that has been written on the environment, but as you may have already guessed, this was possible using the configuration management system itself.

Then why are we still talking about it? We just want to introduce a few new tools that can help us templatize so that we can simply deploy the template in the environment and this makes the process repeatable. (So that we don't have to deploy from the source each time.)

The first one in this list is a tool from HashiCorp called **Packer**. This tool allows us to create customized *virtual machine templates* on a variety of clouds, and it allows customization using a variety of configuration management software.

The second one you need to know about is the Dockerfile. This is used to create Docker container images. If the development is happening for the container environment, the Dockerfile will create a *docker template*, which can be used to deploy the containers.

DevOps or NoOps

Now that we know about the IaaC and the configuration management systems, the next order of business is naturally to see how the enterprises are gearing up toward using these. The enterprises are in essence trying to make the operations team redundant and pass the full responsibility on to the development team, we call this NoOps.

But since that is too far a jump for one to make, the industry decided to make an interim jump, where there will be a common team that will have representation from the development team and the operations teams, but the operations teams have a mandate to use automation/coding in order to create and deliver the configuration; this is called DevOps.

Let's take a look at the responsibility matrix in the traditional, DevOps, and NoOps model:

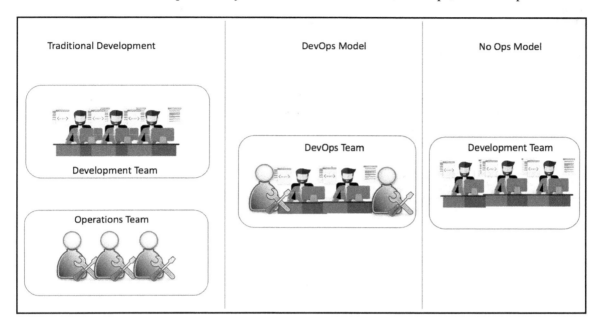

Task	Traditional	DevOps	NoOps
Application architecture	Development team	DevOps team	Development team
Deployment architecture	Operations team	DevOps team	Development team
Deploying servers	Operations team	DevOps team—using IaC/API calls	Development team
Development of applications	Development team	DevOps team	Development team
Deployment of applications	Operations team	DevOps team—using configuration management / template creation tools	Development team
Upgrades	Operations team	DevOps team—using configuration management tools	Development team

Do remember that while the NoOps seems like the Utopian state, most enterprises may not aspire to be there if the goal is agility. The agility is comparable in both the DevOps and NoOps mode as both use the automated systems.

In addition to the agility, if the goal is cost saving (for example, cost of salaries), then the enterprises may push through to the NoOps stage.

 There are other terminologies such as DevSecOps or SecDevOps, these simply signify the addition of the security components and principles into the development stages itself.

Let's take a look at the process with the full view of all the tools in action:

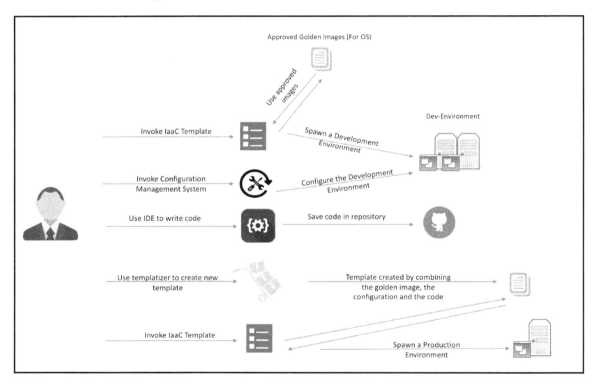

 Note that use of a templatizer is not mandatory. We can use the configuration management system to directly deliver the code after the IaaC template has created the environment.

In a real-life scenario, the public cloud providers give us the ability to use web hooks, and services to create the CI/CD pipeline, in which the code which can be committed in a repository (such as GitHub) will be directly pulled down to the environment and installed, thereby not needing the *templatizer*.

Templatizer has been covered in this book to cover most of the possibilities. We should also be informed that several developer services offered by the public clouds actually also support on-premise systems, thereby making it naively hybrid.

One such example is AWS CodeDeploy, which uses an agent to directly deploy the code from the repository on to the instances (on-premise or on EC2). This can simplify the deployment aspect of the code greatly.

IaaC with Terraform

Armed with the information, we know that there are several ways to address the **Development Operations** (**DevOps**) and this largely varies depending on the kind of the organization, the processes that they use, and the kind of applications they develop.

However, we know that IaaC is a great way to be able to deploy the needed virtual environment (or stack) for the development or production. We also know that each service down cloud seems to have its own IaaC service and even its own format. So, when we are dealing with a hybrid cloud, we will need to create and manage two sets of IaaC templates with two different syntaxes in order to create it.

In our example, where we use a hybrid cloud of OpenStack and AWS, we will need to manage Heat and CloudFormation templates and also know the nuances of both of the IaaC templates. This becomes an operational challenge and in order to solve this, Terraform (https://www.terraform.io) was introduced. This tool has both a community version and an enterprise version.

This system abstracts the IaaC by allowing you to write in a common language to be able to provision on multiple clouds and thereby making it perfect for our hybrid cloud. Read the use cases that it supports by navigating to https://www.terraform.io/intro/use-cases.html.

The current version of Terraform supports over 70 providers. You can refer to the full list at `https://www.terraform.io/docs/providers/`:

Alicloud	Archive	AWS
Azure	Bitbucket	CenturyLinkCloud
Chef	Circonus	Cloudflare
CloudScale.ch	CloudStack	Cobbler
Consul	Datadog	DigitalOcean
DNS	DNSMadeEasy	DNSimple
Docker	Dyn	External
Fastly	GitHub	Gitlab
Google Cloud	Grafana	Heroku
HTTP	Icinga2	Ignition
InfluxDB	Kubernetes	Librato
Local	Logentries	LogicMonitor
Mailgun	MySQL	New Relic
Nomad	NS1	Null
1&1	Oracle Public Cloud	OpenStack
OpenTelekomCloud	OpsGenie	OVH
Packet	PagerDuty	Palo Alto Networks
PostgreSQL	PowerDNS	ProfitBricks
RabbitMQ	Rancher	Random
Rundeck	Scaleway	SoftLayer
StatusCake	Spotinst	Template
Terraform	Terraform Enterprise	TLS
Triton	UltraDNS	Vault
VMware vCloud Director	VMware vSphere	

The provider concept in Terraform means that Terraform can make API calls to that system, and thereby is able to provision resources on that system.

As an example, Terraform can be used to create an EC2 instance on AWS and a nova machine on OpenStack and create the DNS entries for them on DNSimple.

Installing Terraform

The installation is straightforward as Terraform is distributed in a binary form, so we don't have to compile it at our end. The following are the major steps in installing it:

- Download ZIP
- Unzip the download
- Place the binary file in your path

Since this is a management tool, we will put this on the management server that we used to run the Juju scripts. You can choose to run this from your own management server. The management server I am using is an Ubuntu 16.04 LTS and the steps for that are given as follows, for everything else. You can follow the instructions at `https://www.terraform.io/intro/getting-started/install.html`.

> If you don't have a management server, you can download Terraform and use it from your macOS/Windows PC. However, it is recommended that the directory where we will store the IaC templates and the configuration files (as it will contain sensitive data—like access/secret key of the cloud) be protected and backed up.

```
alokshrivastwa@instance-1:~$ mkdir terraform
alokshrivastwa@instance-1:~$ cd terraform/
alokshrivastwa@instance-1:~/terraform$ wget https://releases.hashicorp.com/terraform/0.11.3/terraform_0.11.3_linux_amd64.zip?_ga=2.70404179.2143567178.1
518149145-716135120.1517109232 -O terraformDownload.zip
--2018-02-09 09:15:04--  https://releases.hashicorp.com/terraform/0.11.3/terraform_0.11.3_linux_amd64.zip?_ga=2.70404179.2143567178.1518149145-716135120
.1517109232
Resolving releases.hashicorp.com (releases.hashicorp.com)... 151.101.1.183, 151.101.65.183, 151.101.129.183, ...
Connecting to releases.hashicorp.com (releases.hashicorp.com)|151.101.1.183|:443... connected.
HTTP request sent, awaiting response... 200 OK
Length: 16466291 (16M) [application/zip]
Saving to: 'terraformDownload.zip'

terraformDownload.zip           100%[===================================================================================>]  15.70M  24.1MB/s    in 0.7s

2018-02-09 09:15:05 (24.1 MB/s) - 'terraformDownload.zip' saved [16466291/16466291]

alokshrivastwa@instance-1:~/terraform$
alokshrivastwa@instance-1:~/terraform$
alokshrivastwa@instance-1:~/terraform$
alokshrivastwa@instance-1:~/terraform$ ls
terraformDownload.zip
alokshrivastwa@instance-1:~/terraform$ unzip terraformDownload.zip
Archive:  terraformDownload.zip
  inflating: terraform
alokshrivastwa@instance-1:~/terraform$
alokshrivastwa@instance-1:~/terraform$ ls
terraform  terraformDownload.zip
alokshrivastwa@instance-1:~/terraform$
```

We create a directory and download the file using `wget`. The resulting file is a ZIP and we use the unzip command to uncover the executable:

```
mkdir terraform
cd terraform

wget \
https://releases.hashicorp.com/terraform/0.11.3/terraform_0.11.3_linux_amd6
```

```
4.zip?_ga=2.70404179.2143567178.1518149145-716135120.1517109232 -O
terraformDownload.zip

unzip terraformDownload.zip
```

 Note that the download link was taken from `https://www.terraform.io/downloads.html`.

Now, the Terraform executable is ready to be used, but since it is not in the path, we will copy it to a directory which is in the path or simply add the current directory in the path.

```
sudo cp terraform /usr/local/bin
```

Once this is completed, we can use the Terraform command without specifying the location of the executable.

Configuring and using Terraform

Terraform configurations are in **HashiCorp Configuration Language** (HCL) and can also be JSON formatted. The configuration files normally end with `.tf` and they can be used to configure various things.

 Read `https://www.terraform.io/docs/configuration/syntax.html` for understanding the syntax in detail.

In the current sample, we will initialize the two cloud providers for us (AWS and OpenStack) and create a simple IaaC code, which will create resources in both the clouds.

 Refer to the `https://www.terraform.io/docs/providers/index.html` for the configuration for each provider.

We will create two files for the providers `prov-os.tf` and `prov-aws.tf`. The filenames can be anything as long as they end with the `.tf` extension. By default, the Terraform will load all the `.tf` files in the current directory.

The contents of `prov-os.tf` will have the provider configuration for our OpenStack (use the same credentials from our DevStack installation that has been used so far):

```
provider "openstack" {
 user_name = "admin"
 tenant_name = "admin"
 password = "pass4adminUser"
 auth_url = "http://10.128.0.3:5000/v2.0"
 region = "RegionOne"
}
```

The contents of the `prov-aws.tf` will be as follows:

```
provider "aws" {
 access_key = "<Enter Access Key Here>"
 secret_key = "<Enter Secret Key Here>"
 region = "us-east-1"
}
```

It is good practice not to save the access key and secret key in the script. If the script doesn't find them here, the script will look in the `~/.aws/credentials` file. However, in our case, we are keeping it in the file as the entire directory will have to be secured anyway.

We can also choose to export them into the environment variable, where Terraform is running:

```
$ export AWS_ACCESS_KEY_ID="<Enter Access Key>"
$ export AWS_SECRET_ACCESS_KEY="<Enter Secret Key>"
$ export AWS_DEFAULT_REGION="us-east-1"
```

Once the providers have been created, we can initialize the Terraform working directory using the following command:

```
terraform init
```

This will download the provider plugins and store it in a hidden folder `.terraform`:

```
alokshrivastwa@instance-1:~/terraform$ terraform init

Initializing provider plugins...
- Checking for available provider plugins on https://releases.hashicorp.com...
- Downloading plugin for provider "aws" (1.8.0)...
- Downloading plugin for provider "openstack" (1.2.0)...

The following providers do not have any version constraints in configuration,
so the latest version was installed.

To prevent automatic upgrades to new major versions that may contain breaking
changes, it is recommended to add version = "..." constraints to the
corresponding provider blocks in configuration, with the constraint strings
suggested below.

* provider.aws: version = "~> 1.8"
* provider.openstack: version = "~> 1.2"

Terraform has been successfully initialized!

You may now begin working with Terraform. Try running "terraform plan" to see
any changes that are required for your infrastructure. All Terraform commands
should now work.

If you ever set or change modules or backend configuration for Terraform,
rerun this command to reinitialize your working directory. If you forget, other
commands will detect it and remind you to do so if necessary.
alokshrivastwa@instance-1:~/terraform$
alokshrivastwa@instance-1:~/terraform$
alokshrivastwa@instance-1:~/terraform$
alokshrivastwa@instance-1:~/terraform$ ls
prov-aws.tf  prov-os.tf
alokshrivastwa@instance-1:~/terraform$ ls -la
total 20
drwxrwxr-x  3 alokshrivastwa alokshrivastwa 4096 Feb  9 16:56 .
drwxr-xr-x 10 alokshrivastwa alokshrivastwa 4096 Feb  9 16:56 ..
-rw-rw-r--  1 alokshrivastwa alokshrivastwa  121 Feb  9 16:56 prov-aws.tf
-rw-rw-r--  1 alokshrivastwa alokshrivastwa  162 Feb  9 16:56 prov-os.tf
drwxrwxr-x  3 alokshrivastwa alokshrivastwa 4096 Feb  9 16:56 .terraform
```

Once this is complete, we are ready to create the IaC code. The resources and definitions can be found on the provider page `https://www.terraform.io/docs/providers/aws/index.html`.

In the following code, we will simply instantiate an AWS EC2 machine. Create a file in the system called `example-iaac.tf`. The contents of the file are as follows:

```
resource "aws_instance" "deployment-1" {
  ami = "ami-b374d5a5"
  instance_type = "t2.micro"
}
```

The file simply tells Terraform that a resource of the type `aws_instance` with the name `deployment-1` will be created with the AMI ID and instance type as shown in the filename.

Once we create, we will execute the `terraform plan` command, which will tell us the changes that Terraform is going to perform:

```
alokshrivastwa@instance-1:~/terraform$ terraform plan
Refreshing Terraform state in-memory prior to plan...
The refreshed state will be used to calculate this plan, but will not be
persisted to local or remote state storage.


------------------------------------------------------------------------


An execution plan has been generated and is shown below.
Resource actions are indicated with the following symbols:
  + create

Terraform will perform the following actions:

  + aws_instance.deployment-1
      id:                             <computed>
      ami:                            "ami-b374d5a5"
      associate_public_ip_address:    <computed>
      availability_zone:              <computed>
      ebs_block_device.#:             <computed>
      ephemeral_block_device.#:       <computed>
      instance_state:                 <computed>
      instance_type:                  "t2.micro"
      ipv6_address_count:             <computed>
      ipv6_addresses.#:               <computed>
      key_name:                       <computed>
      network_interface.#:            <computed>
      network_interface_id:           <computed>
      placement_group:                <computed>
      primary_network_interface_id:   <computed>
      private_dns:                    <computed>
      private_ip:                     <computed>
      public_dns:                     <computed>
      public_ip:                      <computed>
      root_block_device.#:            <computed>
      security_groups.#:              <computed>
      source_dest_check:              "true"
      subnet_id:                      <computed>
      tenancy:                        <computed>
      volume_tags.%:                  <computed>
      vpc_security_group_ids.#:       <computed>


Plan: 1 to add, 0 to change, 0 to destroy.

------------------------------------------------------------------------
```

As we can notice, we could have passed several arguments in the resource section like network interface, `subnet_id`, and so on. Read the documentation for more details at `https://www.terraform.io/docs/index.html`.

Once you have validated the task, execute the `terraform apply` command to create the infrastructure.

 In order to change the configuration, simply change this file and execute the `terraform apply` command again to modify the configuration.

Note that this was a brief introduction to Terraform. Terraform can be used to create several resources and types across multiple providers. You also view the joint webinar by HashiCorp and AWS explaining Terraform at `https://www.youtube.com/watch?v=TFLQcgZr0no`.

Configuration management using Ansible

Now that we have dealt with the IaaC system, we will look at the configuration management system. We have chosen Ansible (`http://ansible.com`) simply because, like Terraform, it also works on a client-only model.

We will be using the same management machine in order to install Ansible. It logs into the servers that it manages using SSH (for Linux) and WinRM (for Windows). The configuration management definitions for Ansible is called a playbook and there are several of them available on the internet.

Installing Ansible

The installation of Ansible can be done using the `yum` or **aptitude package manager** (**apt**) depending on the operating system.

Since our management server is Ubuntu, we will use the following commands:

```
sudo apt-get install software-properties-common
sudo apt-add-repository ppa:ansible/ansible
sudo apt-get update
sudo apt-get install ansible
```

Once the Ansible is installed, we are ready to use them by merely modifying a few files.

Configuring Ansible and a sample playbook

Now, we will perform the following steps:

- Create a file with server IP address and group name (Ansible hosts file)
- Create a playbook to install Apache and start it

By default, Ansible expects the Ansible hosts file at the location `/etc/ansible/hosts` and it expects its configuration in a file called `ansible.cfg` in the current directory.

The contents of the Ansible host file (`/etc/ansible/hosts`) is as follows:

```
[sample-group]
10.128.0.3
```

This simply means that there is a group called `sample-group` and it has only one server (`10.128.0.3`). We will now write a playbook file in order to install the Apache and start it.

Create an `apache-playbook.yml` file:

```
---
- hosts: sample-group
  remote_user: alokshrivastwa
  become: yes
  become_method: sudo
  tasks:
    - name: "Install Apache"
      apt: name={{ item }} state=present
      with_items:
        - apache2

    - name: "Turn on Apache to run on boot"
      service: name={{ item }} state=started enabled=yes
      with_items:
        - apache2
```

We have simply specified that the username to be used to connect to the servers is `sample-group`.

We will execute the `ansible-playbook` command to run this playbook. Since we have not set up passwordless SSH, we have to use the `--ask-pass` switch to provide the password:

```
ansible-playbook apache-playbook.yml -u alokshrivastwa --ask-pass
```

We will see that the Ansible playbook is successfully run and Apache has been installed:

```
alokshrivastwa@instance-1:~$ ansible-playbook apache-playbook.yml -u alokshrivastwa --ask-pass
SSH password:

PLAY ***************************************************************************

TASK [setup] ******************************************************************
ok: [10.128.0.3]

TASK [Install Apache] *********************************************************
changed: [10.128.0.3] => (item=[u'apache2'])

TASK [Turn on Apache] *********************************************************
changed: [10.128.0.3] => (item=apache2)

PLAY RECAP ********************************************************************
10.128.0.3                 : ok=3    changed=2    unreachable=0    failed=0
```

Normally, we will use passwordless SSH to be able to log in to the systems. Follow the link `https://medium.com/@visualskyrim/ansible-playbook-deploy-the-public-key-to-remote-hosts-da3f3b4b5481` to deploy the public key so that the passwordless login can be deployed enmasse to the servers that we need to manage.

Ansible is really powerful and is being used to manage network devices in addition to servers. It can even work with clouds such as AWS to deploy servers. Read the full documentation for the use cases and how to work with them.

Summary

While every organization may have a slightly different place, the tools that we have in our toolbelt will help us operate a DevOps environment and management style. The tools that were mentioned can be substituted with an equivalent, but the architecture and mode of doing the operations is covered in this chapter.

In the next chapter, we will get into the operations mode and discuss the monitoring and graphing aspects of the hybrid cloud.

10
Monitoring the Hybrid Cloud

If you have ever run, or worked in an IT operations environment, you will agree when I say that one of the key aspects of running operations is monitoring and being proactive rather than being reactive.

However, in the hybrid cloud world, this monitoring becomes of paramount importance. The reason for it is we start treating the infrastructure as *cattle* and most of the time, we don't even try and troubleshoot for the issue, but rather *rip and replace* the infrastructure. Some of this is actually automatic. For instance, if a Kubernetes pod hosting an application goes down due to the underlying infrastructure, the system will simply spawn a new one in its place and all of this monitoring is essential.

Since you are reading this book, I think it is safe to assume that you are either planning or implementing the creation/optimization or operation of a hybrid cloud environment. In that respect, you will appreciate that in order to go to self-healing applications, monitoring plays a key role.

The traditional concepts in monitoring

Monitoring is a problem that has been solved in many different ways for many different levels of stack. Let's take a look at different demographics of monitoring:

- Availability monitoring (up/down monitoring)
- Performance monitoring (time series—CPU, memory, utilization, and so on)

In the infrastructure side of things, availability monitoring and performance monitoring are both used, but the application side is a little heavy on the performance monitoring as the availability of the application is monitored on the infrastructure level itself by the load balancers and the likes.

The following diagram shows the different protocols that are generally used in monitoring systems of different types:

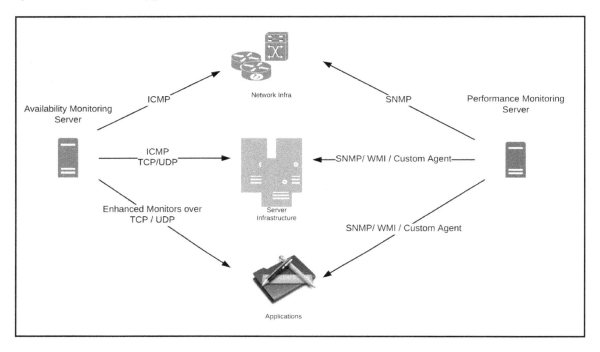

Availability monitoring

This is the simplest kind of monitoring, which marks the object that is being monitored as either *up* or *down*. This is generally done using several protocols such as ICMP (ICMP_ECHO) and sometimes even TCP and UDP (or enhanced verification on these).

In most cases, this is done using a *poll* method, which means the monitoring system sends a probe to the server that is being monitored. If the probe fails a few times, the system is then marked as down. Availability monitoring is agentless and relies on the network stack that is running by default.

Ideally, a poll mechanism contains the following settings:

- **Polling interval**: This is the interval at which the probes are sent
- **Timeout**: This is the time since the last successful response to consider that the system is down

A subset of this monitoring can also be done by the SNMP protocol's trap feature, where we don't keep polling continuously, but if an event happens, the device lets us know it's using the SNMP trap feature. While this mechanism is available, not many system administrators use and rely on this feature alone.

The following screenshot is from the tool OpenNMS, which shows the availability monitoring events to show the kind of monitoring we are talking about:

Ack	ID ▼ Severity	Node Ackd	Interface Ackd Time	Service	Count	Last Event Time	First Event Time
☐	7 Critical [+] [-]	172.20.1.201 [+] [-] Node 172.20.1.201 is down.	0.0.0.0 [+] [-]		3	4/21/05 6:05:41 PM [<] [>]	4/20/05 6:36:26 PM [<] [>]
☐	15 Critical [+] [-]	172.20.1.200 [+] [-] Node 172.20.1.200 is down.	0.0.0.0 [+] [-]		1	4/22/05 6:26:21 PM [<] [>]	4/22/05 6:26:21 PM [<] [>]
☐	12 Critical [+] [-]	David-Hustaces-Computer.local [+] [-] Node David-Hustaces-Computer.local is down.	0.0.0.0 [+] [-]		2	4/22/05 6:26:33 PM [<] [>]	4/22/05 2:35:43 PM [<] [>]
☐	3 Major [+] [-]	barbrady.opennms.com [+] [-] HTTP outage identified on interface 172.20.1.11.	172.20.1.11 [+] [-]	HTTP [+] [-]	2	4/20/05 5:25:51 PM [<] [>]	4/20/05 5:10:43 PM [<] [>]
☐	4 Major [+] [-]	barbrady.opennms.com [+] [-] HTTPS outage identified on interface 172.20.1.11.	172.20.1.11 [+] [-]	HTTPS [+] [-]	2	4/20/05 5:25:53 PM [<] [>]	4/20/05 5:10:44 PM [<] [>]
☐	11 Major [+] [-]	barbrady.opennms.com [+] [-] HTTP-8080 outage identified on interface 172.20.1.11.	172.20.1.11 [+] [-]	HTTP-8080 [+] [-]	1	4/22/05 10:58:38 AM [<] [>]	4/22/05 10:58:38 AM [<] [>]
☐	16 Major [+] [-]	cartman.opennms.com [+] [-] HTTP outage identified on interface 172.20.1.10.	172.20.1.10 [+] [-]	HTTP [+] [-]	1	4/22/05 8:09:44 PM [<] [>]	4/22/05 8:09:44 PM [<] [>]
☐	9 Major [+] [-]	172.20.1.201 [+] [-] SSH outage identified on interface 172.20.1.201.	172.20.1.201 [+] [-]	SSH [+] [-]	23	4/23/05 7:44:32 AM [<] [>]	4/21/05 3:57:30 PM [<] [>]
☐	8 Normal [+] [-]	mrmakey.opennms.com [+] [-] Linksys Event: @out TCP from 172.20.1.204:65247 to 198.128.246.160(198.128.246.160):80.	172.20.1.1 [+] [-]		38705	4/23/05 11:14:14 AM [<] [>]	4/19/05 4:45:10 PM [<] [>]
☐	6 Cleared [+] [-]	barbrady.opennms.com [+] [-] The HTTPS outage on interface 172.20.1.11 has been cleared. Service is restored.	172.20.1.11 [+] [-]	HTTPS [+] [-]	2	4/20/05 5:27:56 PM [<] [>]	4/20/05 5:20:53 PM [<] [>]

Results 1-10 of 16
1 2 Next Last

10 alarms   Acknowledge Alarms | Select All | Reset

Having understood the nature of availability monitoring, let's see the ways in which it is performed.

ICMP monitoring

This simply implies sending an ICMP echo packet, also known as **network ping**, and waiting for a response for a predefined period. The packet is stateless and can travel through a firewall. However, some firewalls decide to block it from a security standpoint, but ICMP is almost always available inside a data center. The packets don't take much to process (comparatively) and so don't cause much load on the server.

In the olden days, there was an attack where several thousand ICMP requests would flood the memory of the system, thereby disallowing credible requests and creating a denial of service attack. This kind of pinging was called the **ping of death**.

While most devices are immune to this attack, ICMP to this date is disallowed (where possible) from an external network to prevent this and also prevent **footprinting**—finding out information about the network estate before an attack.

The response to ICMP simply implies that the network stack in the *node* that is being monitored is operational and no information about the applications that are running can be inferred.

TCP/UDP monitoring

The TCP/UDP monitoring is a little more advanced than the simple ICMP echo that we saw in the previous section. In this, a connection is sent to a port on the network stack and checked to see whether the port is opened.

A network port is nothing more than a *memory buffer* associated with a number in the network stack. Once an application needs to *listen* for the network traffic, it makes a call to the operating system kernel, for a number and a memory location.

The kernel assigns the number and memory location and also makes the TCP/IP stack aware of it. Once someone sends a packet to that port, the TCP/IP stack traversing through various layers gets the *segment* and puts it on the memory location.

It then becomes the application's responsibility to read from the memory location and also clears it. Hence, if the application doesn't exist, the port will not be open and listening.

The following diagram shows this concept in a simplified manner from opening the port and storing the data in it:

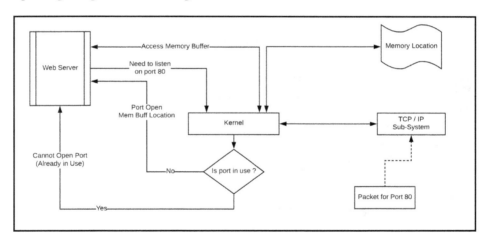

Checking a *port* that is opened confirms whether a certain application is running on the server. For example, if TCP port 80 is opened, chances are that the web server is running on the node. This is slightly better than just checking whether the network stack is running.

As you might already be aware, the TCP health check takes about three packets to establish the connection with the help of several flags. (The TCP is beyond the purview of the book and hence is not been covered in detail.)

The first packet in establishing whether a TCP connection we send is with the SYN (synchronize) flag set, which is also called SYN packet. The server then responds by sending its own SYN and acknowledging our SYN (SYN-ACK packet), and finally, we acknowledge the SYN of the server (ACK packet). This process also initializes the sequence numbers, the window size, and so on and so forth.

In order to monitor a port, we can simply make a connection by sending a SYN packet to the node on a TCP port that we want to monitor. If we get a SYN-ACK back, then the port is listening.

The advantage is that this monitoring is allowed from external firewalls as well, as we are trying to emulate a real-world example, which means the customers trying to connect to our web servers will have to do this.

TCP monitoring is done in one of the following two ways:

- **TCP half-open**: In this, we send the SYN packet. When the SYN-ACK comes, we simply don't respond to this. The server, in this case, keeps the connection open for some time, waiting for our ACK packet.
- **TCP full**: In this, when the SYN-ACK packet comes, we respond with a **finalize** (**FIN**) or **reset** (**RST**) to tell the server to terminate the connection.

TCP full is better for the node that is being monitored, than half-open once the RST flag is sent. The node releases the memory that it allocated for the connection.

TCP half-open is better for the monitoring server, as it doesn't bother sending another packet and gets on its way of monitoring other servers.

Enhanced monitoring

With the TCP and UDP monitoring, we went one step further than the ICMP monitoring; however, if the application is *hung*, the TCP port might be open, but the application is not picking up data from the memory buffer.

In order to verify that the application itself may be working, we use enhanced monitoring, where the application is asked to do perform a certain task and then the response is checked to see whether everything matches, and then it is considered up or down.

As an example, let's assume we are monitoring the web server, and we create a page called `testmonitor.html` with the content `Webserver is UP`. The enhanced monitor will perform an HTTP GET in order to get the page, and can validate the content.

 The enhanced verification is mostly used in load balancers trying to absolutely make sure that the node is up and serving the applications as intended.

SNMP-based availability monitoring

Availability monitoring can also be done using SNMP; however, when SNMP is involved, we don't merely do availability and due to this reason, it has been covered in the next section.

In summary, availability monitoring is an event (which is up or down) and is used in several places, such as in the load balancer monitor, to mark the servers up or down and in general operations to create a ticket in an ITSM tool, which allows the operations team to react to the event.

Performance monitoring

Performance monitoring is also done in the poll model, but this one generally needs an agent. It could be a standard SNMP agent or the monitoring servers agent. At the infrastructure level, performance monitoring is done to get information about CPU, memory, network utilization, and so on, and in the case of applications, several parameters such as heap size and number of connections are of interest.

Do remember that the protocols themselves don't create graphs, but the monitoring system receiving the information internally stores it in a time series database and allows for the alerts to be triggered if there are thresholds breached.

The following is a dashboard from Cacti, an open source product showing the CPU utilization monitoring:

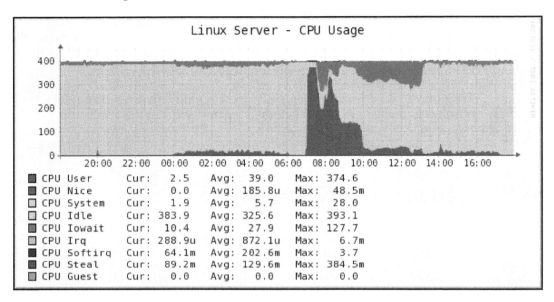

In most cases, the metrics for these systems are generally extracted using SNMP and WMI (in case of Windows), and some of the tool makers could write their own agents that can run inside of an operating system.

SNMP monitoring

Simple Network Management Protocol (**SNMP**) is a wide-spread protocol used to retrieve the metrics in a client-server setting.

The nodes that are being monitored generally have an *SNMP agent* installed on them. They generally listen to UDP port 161. The SNMP server can then make requests to them for certain information.

The information that is being asked for is encoded in a series of numbers called the **object identifier** (**OID**). The OIDs are organized in a tree fashion for extensibility and ease of use. Since the OID is a tree, it is also traversed like one, which means you can request for all the entries under a certain branch, go to the next entry, go to previous entry, and so on. In order to see the OID tree, visit: http://www.oid-info.com/cgi-bin/display?tree=0.

The tree structure allows for the addition of new branches by the manufacturer, so that information pertaining to their product can be added. For example, a certain printer manufacturer decides to expose the ink/toner levels of the printer; they can add the OID in their branch. The OID for standard systems are also defined.

For example, the OIDs for hostname, description, and so on have already been defined and so manufacturers can simply use these. Some sample OIDs are shown as follows and the corresponding tree structure is given (all of them belong to the same branch):

- 1.3.6.1.2.1.1.1: sysDescr
- 1.3.6.1.2.1.1.2: sysObjectID
- 1.3.6.1.2.1.1.3: sysUpTime
- 1.3.6.1.2.1.1.4: sysContact
- 1.3.6.1.2.1.1.5: sysName
- 1.3.6.1.2.1.1.6: sysLocation
- 1.3.6.1.2.1.1.7: sysServices

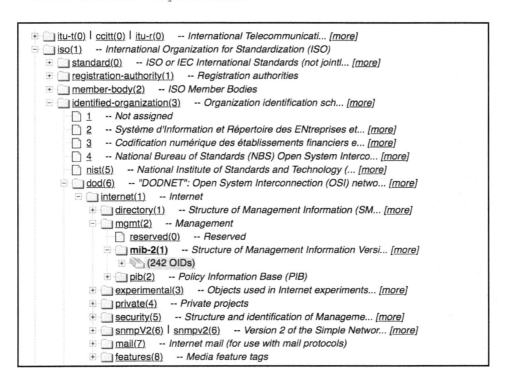

The SNMP protocol has three versions, and most people use version 2 or 3 in order to make calls. While the SNMP version 3 is more secure (due to encryption and the like), SNMP v2c still takes the center stage most times.

SNMP also allows for SNMP traps or events that can be sent by the nodes directly to the SNMP trap receiver. The following diagram shows the conceptual operation of both the SNMP poll and the trap:

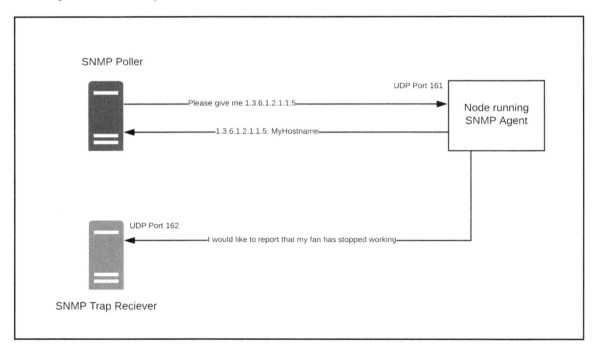

As we can clearly see, this method allows us to get more insight into the server when compared to what availability monitoring allowed us to do.

WMI monitoring and custom agent monitoring

Windows Management Instrumentation (**WMI**) is used in order to do the monitoring of Windows Server alone. While there is no reason that SNMP cannot be used, Microsoft introduced WMI to natively work with several of its operating systems. It uses RPC for communication, but the basic idea and concepts remain the same.

Several monitoring systems can use their own custom agent for monitoring. While the concept doesn't vary much, they can do the following:

- Make the agent smart enough so that it sends data to the monitoring server, than having the monitoring server poll for the data. This helps the monitoring server become more event-based.
- Add some code, which performs some specific kind of monitoring. For example, one can teach the agent to provide deep insights about running the application—for example heap memory, variable locking, and so on. Most application monitoring systems use this mode.

Monitoring the hybrid cloud

Armed with the knowledge about monitoring, let's look at how this changes in the hybrid cloud world or even just the cloud world. Can we not use the same systems that we were using in the traditional environment to monitor the new one?

The answer is yes, for the systems that it was made for monitoring, we can. This means there is no difference in whether we monitored a virtual or physical machine on premises or on the cloud; we can use the same mechanism.

However, is this recommended? The answer is, not really. If you ask why, let's take a look at the main reasons behind it, which are listed as follows:

- The cloud platform already monitors some of the resources (for the sake of autoscaling and the like); the old system of monitoring doesn't support these
- There are new services that are being used and the old system doesn't know how to monitor these systems (as an example of containers)
- There have been several improvements in the new tools to be more optimized, and so we will be losing on these features if we did the monitoring in the same way

But, then the question begs, are the new monitoring systems doing the things way differently than the previous ones? The answer to this question is also a *no*.

The new age monitoring systems do what the old ones used to do (maybe a little better); however, the key difference is that the new systems are aware of the underlying platforms and they can take the metrics from there. In the case of the cloud, they can take the metrics from the cloud provider, while in the case of the containers, they can take the metrics from the container host.

The other aspect of monitoring that has evolved beyond the traditional monitoring is the concept of **log monitoring** with products such as Splunk, ELK Stack, and Graylog.

To explain the log monitoring in the most simplest way, it is taking the logs of several kinds of devices and storing them in a same searchable location. This helps in correlation and getting the insights from the logs. This is what is also being fed to several analytics engines in order to diagnose, and to some extent, even predict the outages/issues in the infrastructure and applications.

There are several new age monitoring solutions, but as we have done throughout the book, we will be looking at the best open source product in the class of new age monitoring systems.

Prometheus

Prometheus (`https://prometheus.io`) is one of the top new generation open source monitoring systems. This system possesses one of the best time series databases among other features. This tool supports multiple cloud backends and supports a dimensional data model.

At the core, the Prometheus system scrapes HTTP endpoints and can get metrics. This then stores it in its own time series database. The tool by itself doesn't provide a dashboard, so we will also be using Grafana in order to provide us with the required dashboard. It also uses a separate alert manager in order to generate events in case the thresholds are breached. Together, this system is called **Grafana-Alertmanager-Prometheus** (**GAP**), and is being used extensively in a cloud scenario.

The implementation architecture of Prometheus

Let's take a look at how the system is implemented and how it can be set up as a monitoring solution. The Prometheus system can talk to the HTTP endpoints, so the conceptual architecture is as follows:

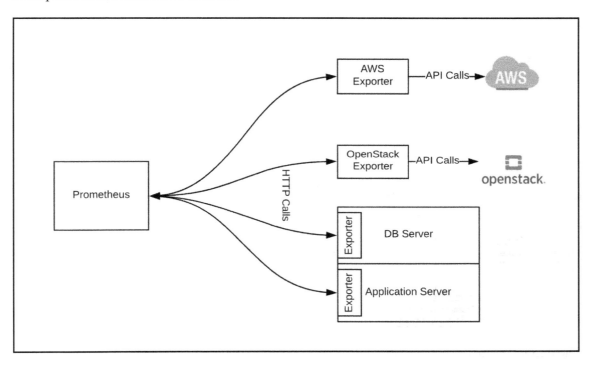

Taking a look at the overall architecture, including the Grafana and Alertmanager, the architecture looks as shown in the following diagram, which is from the official Prometheus GitHub page (`https://github.com/prometheus/prometheus`):

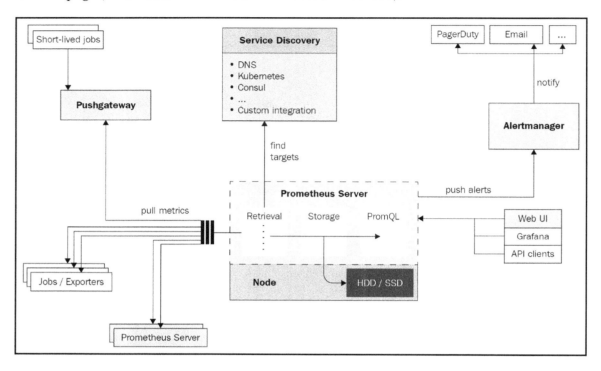

The exporters are akin to agents for the Prometheus as these become the HTTP endpoints for Prometheus to scrape metrics from. These also make Prometheus extremely scalable, robust, and stateless.

The exporters themselves are fairly simple to write, so one can add any kind of exporter that is needed. There are several languages in which the exporters can be written. Read the details about instrumentation of Prometheus at: `https://prometheus.io/docs/instrumenting/clientlibs`.

The available exporters are listed at: `https://prometheus.io/docs/instrumenting/exporters/`.

Installing Prometheus

There are several options available for the installation of the system, right from using the binary directly to the system, using Docker containers, and not to forget, installing it from the source. Refer to the following link for all the available options `https://prometheus.io/docs/prometheus/latest/installation/`.

We will be installing it on the same management server that we are running with (the same place where we ran the Juju, Terraform, and Ansible from). We will then be installing the node and AWS exporter.

The install process is done using the following steps:

1. Download the executable from the **Downloads** page
2. Unzip and move the executable to the appropriate path
3. Create directories
4. Create systemd services for Prometheus

Downloading Prometheus

Go to the downloads page at `https://prometheus.io/download` and get the download link for your distribution. Since we are using Linux, we will use the Linux version (during the writing of the book, the version was 2.1):

```
wget
https://github.com/prometheus/prometheus/releases/download/v2.1.0/prometheu
s-2.1.0.linux-amd64.tar.gz
```

Once downloaded, let's untar and unzip it. This will give us a folder with two subfolders and two executables:

```
tar -xvzf prometheus-2.1.0.linux-amd64.tar.gz
```

Setting up directories

We will now create the relevant directories, users, and move the files:

```
sudo mkdir /etc/prometheus
sudo mkdir /var/lib/prometheus
sudo useradd prometheus

# Moving the executables
sudo cp prometheus-2.1.0.linux-amd64/prometheus /usr/local/bin/
sudo cp prometheus-2.1.0.linux-amd64/promtool /usr/local/bin/
```

```
#Copying the folders
sudo cp -r prometheus-2.1.0.linux-amd64/consoles /etc/prometheus
sudo cp -r prometheus-2.1.0.linux-amd64/console_libraries /etc/prometheus

#Modifying the permissions
sudo chown -R prometheus:prometheus /etc/prometheus
sudo chown -R prometheus:prometheus /var/lib/prometheus/
sudo chown prometheus:prometheus /usr/local/bin/prometheus
sudo chown prometheus:prometheus /usr/local/bin/promtool
```

Setting up startup script

Once this is complete, Prometheus is technically installed and ready to be started. However, we will create a systemd file to start and stop the Prometheus service so that we can use the `systemctl` commands:

```
sudo su

cat <<EOF >> /etc/systemd/system/prometheus.service
[Unit]
Description=Prometheus
Wants=network-online.target
After=network-online.target

[Service]
User=prometheus
Group=prometheus
Type=simple
ExecStart=/usr/local/bin/prometheus \
    --config.file /etc/prometheus/prometheus.yml \
    --storage.tsdb.path /var/lib/prometheus/ \
    --web.console.templates=/etc/prometheus/consoles \
    --web.console.libraries=/etc/prometheus/console_libraries

[Install]
WantedBy=multi-user.target
EOF

exit
```

The preceding code simply mentions that the Prometheus configuration file will be located at `/etc/prometheus/prometheus.yml` and the time series database will be stored at `/var/lib/prometheus/`.

The system will still not start as we have not yet created a configuration file to work with.

Setting up node exporter

This step is optional, but will give you some insight on the concept of exporters. Here, we will install a node exporter, which will help Prometheus scrape through the current node it is running on.

The steps are similar to that of installing the Prometheus system:

1. Download
2. Create directories and users
3. Startup script

For the sake of brevity, we will simply see the following commands:

```
cd ~
wget
https://github.com/prometheus/node_exporter/releases/download/v0.15.2/node_
exporter-0.15.2.linux-amd64.tar.gz
```

Once the download is complete, execute the following commands:

```
tar -xvzf node_exporter-0.15.2.linux-amd64
sudo sudo useradd node_exporter
sudo cp node_exporter-0.15.2.linux-amd64/node_exporter /usr/local/bin
sudo chown node_exporter:node_exporter /usr/local/bin/node_exporter

sudo su

cat <<EOF >> /etc/systemd/system/node_exporter.service
[Unit]
Description=Node Exporter
Wants=network-online.target
After=network-online.target

[Service]

User=node_exporter
Group=node_exporter
Type=simple
ExecStart=/usr/local/bin/node_exporter
[Install]
WantedBy=multi-user.target

EOF

#Lets exit the root mode
exit
```

After the node exporter startup configuration is completed as shown before, we can start it using the following command:

```
sudo systemctl start node_exporter
```

We can see that `node_exporter` is running and listening to port `9100` by default (verify it by typing the `sudo netstat -lnp | grep node_exporter` command).

Now, the node exporter is exporting all the metrics on the HTTP protocol. You can see this by going to: `http://[IP address of your box]:9100/metrics`.

For example, I am simply looking for the CPU metrics from the node (locally) using the following command:

```
curl http://localhost:9100/metrics 2>/dev/null | grep -v "#" | grep cpu
```

If you notice, the same metrics have been found as in the SNMP protocol (notice the screenshot of Cacti in the previous section), but through HTTP.

Configuring Prometheus

Now that we have installed the Prometheus and also installed a node exporter, we will configure Prometheus to collect the data from the different data sources using its configuration file.

Due to the creation of the systemd file in the previous section, the Prometheus configuration will be located at `/etc/prometheus/prometheus.yml`.

This file has a global configuration and configuration for each of the exporters it needs to scrape through:

 Keep in mind that the config is YAML syntax and the spacing is a key aspect (similar to that of Python).

```
sudo su

cat <<EOF >> /etc/prometheus/prometheus.yml
global:
 scrape_interval: 15s
scrape_configs:
 - job_name: 'prometheus_scrape_self'
   scrape_interval: 5s
```

```
    static_configs:
    - targets: ['localhost:9090']
- job_name: 'node_exporter_scraper'
    scrape_interval: 5s
    static_configs:
    - targets: ['localhost:9100']
```

EOF

exit

So, the contents of the configuration file tell the Prometheus server that the `global` config is scraped every 30 seconds. However, we configure the targets to scrape every 10 seconds. We simply put the target as the HTTP endpoint, where an exporter can be found. Since both the exporters (itself and the `node_exporter`) are on the same machine, we have put localhost.

The `job_name` mentioned is a mere tag, so mention something descriptive. For details on all the configuration parameters that are available to us, refer to: `https://prometheus.io/docs/prometheus/latest/configuration/configuration/`.

Once the config is ready, we can start the Prometheus using the following command:

```
sudo systemctl start prometheus
```

Once the system is ready, you can see that the Prometheus is gathering data by navigating to: `http:<IP address of the server>:9090`:

As you can see, we are looking at the node's active memory that Prometheus is scraping and keeping it in its **time series database** (**TSDB**). The graphing done by Prometheus is very rudimentary and hence we will be using Grafana to show the dashboards.

Grafana

Grafana (https://grafana.com) is an open platform, which can be used for dashboarding and analytics. This supports Prometheus as one of the data sources (among many others such as InfluxDB and Graphite).

Installing Grafana

In this section, we will quickly install Grafana and add our Prometheus data source. The installation is fairly straightforward and we will install it on our management box. With regard to instructions for other operating systems, follow this link: http://docs.grafana.org/installation.

Since we are using Ubuntu, the instructions include the following:

1. Download the Debian package
2. Install the Debian package:

```
wget
https://s3-us-west-2.amazonaws.com/grafana-releases/release/grafana
_4.6.3_amd64.deb \
&& sudo apt-get install -y adduser libfontconfig \
&& sudo dpkg -i grafana_4.6.3_amd64.deb
```

The URL can be taken from the download page mentioned previously. Once the installation is complete, we can start the service using the following code:

```
sudo service grafana-server start
```

This starts the server on port 3000. The default credentials are admin/admin:

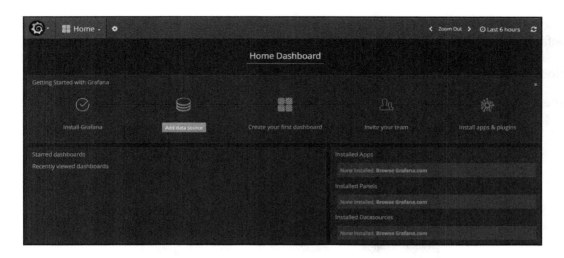

Configuring Grafana to use Prometheus

Once Grafana has been installed, click on **Add Datasource** and provide the **Name** and **URL**. Since we have not enabled any authentication, leave all of that blank:

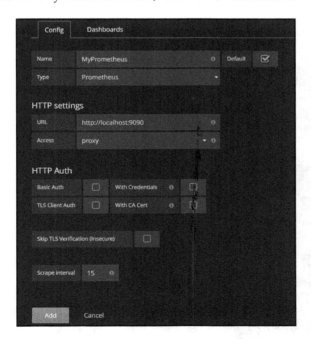

Once the data source has been added, we will create a dashboard. Grafana already gives a default dashboard for Prometheus and we will use that. Navigate to `https://grafana.com/dashboards` to see the predefined dashboards that are available. We will use the **Generic Node** dashboard (`https://grafana.com/dashboards/3297`).

Then, navigate to **Home | Dashboard | Import** and paste the link into the dialog:

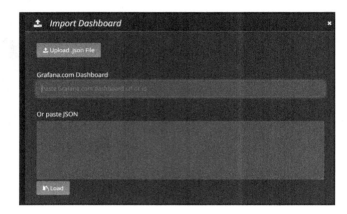

Once the dashboard is ready, you will see it fill with data:

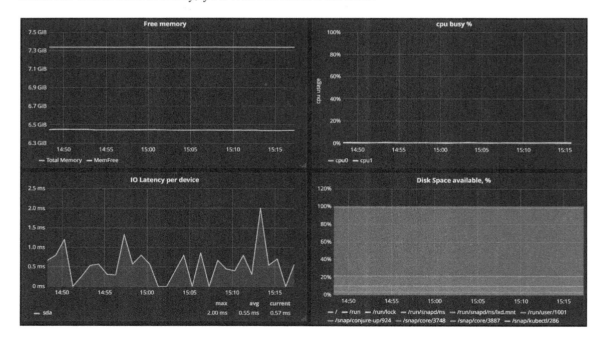

We can create our own dashboards in Grafana, and the information on getting started can be found at: `http://docs.grafana.org/guides/getting_started/`.

Summary

The system that we covered in this chapter needs some more changes to make it production ready, such as securing the Prometheus with user credentials. However, this system is scalable and supports monitoring the systems used in the cloud such as Ceph, HAProxy, OpenStack, and various time series databases.

Prometheus's data model and query language is powerful and allows us to perform a variety of things in a much faster manner. Do remember that in the previous sections (dealing with Prometheus and Grafana), we have not taken into account the ability to generate alerts. Alertmanager (`https://prometheus.io/docs/alerting/alertmanager/`) can be used for these purposes and it supports multiple kinds of notifications and silencing based on tags.

We are almost at the end of the book and in the next and final chapter, we will take a look at some security best practices and some of the compliance standards that are generally followed.

11
Security in a Hybrid Cloud

Security is no longer an optional entity, and it is no longer acceptable to have it as an add-on to the system after building it. It is now built along with the system and is ingrained in it. It isn't wrong to say that it is one of the first things that is discussed when the system is built. Even the DevOps that we learned in the last chapter is becoming SecDevOps (or sometimes DevSecOps), where the *Sec* is for security.

You might consider this as being paranoid, but this paranoia about security is not unfounded; it is simply a fact that the number of attacks is rising and the cost of attacks (including losing data, losing customers, and losing brand value) has become enormous.

In order to get perspective on the number of attacks, according to some of the numbers given by the FBI, 4,000 ransomware attacks happen *every day* (which is a 300% increase from 2015) and the damage has increased to *US $5 billion* ($325 million in 2015), as mentioned in the report at `https://www.fbi.gov/file-repository/ransomware-prevention-and-response-for-cisos.pdf/view`.

The organizations are getting 17,000 malware attacks per week, and only 4% are even triaged, according to Ponemon Institute's research (`http://www.ponemon.org/blog/the-cost-of-malware-containment`).

Even if you are not into cybersecurity, last year we heard about the *WannaCry* ransomware and the havoc it unleashed on unsuspecting people, and hence it is imperative that we have a grasp of the fundamentals and security concepts that we need to keep in mind while architecting the cloud for our use.

Components of security

Security is such a vast topic that even a book to cover it will fall short, let alone a chapter. In this section, we will discuss the base components of security and its definitions.

The CIA triad

The core of information security mainly focuses on the CIA triad, which stands for confidentiality, integrity, and availability of data.

Confidentiality

The data confidentiality principle dictates that access should be allowed only on a need-to-know basis, which means, by default, block all access and only open access when necessary.

Let's take a banking example to elucidate the principles. Say someone comes into the bank and requests to know your bank balance, and is successful. This would be considered a breach in confidentiality.

Integrity

The principle of data integrity is to protect the data from being modified in an unauthorized way while at rest or in motion. The prevention and detection of data tampering falls under this.

Extending the same bank example, say you have given instructions to the bank to transfer $100 to person X, and these instructions are modified to say you want $10,000 to be transferred to a third party; this would be considered a breach of data integrity.

Availability

This simply means that systems should be made in a way such that the possibility of denial of service reduces so that the availability of the system is improved.

Again, using the same bank example, say you are standing in a queue to make some transactions in the bank, and there are people in front of you who are simply flirting with the teller and thereby wasting your time to such an extent that you are unable to perform the business you are there for. That would be considered a breach in availability.

Tools to protect against the breaches

In order to ensure that the CIA triad remains valid, we need to reduce the surface area of the attack and also look at some protection strategies. The systems that are implemented for this are mentioned next:

- Implementing **Identity and Access Management (IAM)**
- Implementing data encryption at rest and in motion
- Implementing network perimeter security—firewalls, IDS, IPS, proxies, and so on
- Implementing host controls—antivirus, anti-malware, and so on
- Implementing high availability and disaster recovery
- Implementing detection mechanisms
- Minimizing shared infrastructure

Now, each of these can be implemented using several products; however, we will look at the concepts with some of the product examples that can help us implement them.

IAM systems

There are several IAM systems available on the market. The primary objective of these systems is to ensure that proper **authentication, authorization, and accounting (AAA)** is done for all the user and computer resources.

Some examples of products are Active Directory, **Azure Active Directory** (**AAD**), AWS Active Directory, and LDAP.

IAM systems are also paired with some of the key management systems to provide access to certain keys which are required to decrypt data for that user.

Data encryption in rest and in motion

Data encryption is the process of making the data unreadable. The encryption is done either with symmetric-key cryptography (for example, AES, 3DES, and so on) or asymmetric-key cryptography (RSA, ECC, and so on).

Data, once encrypted, can only be decrypted by the relevant key by preventing unauthorized access to data. There are two types of encryption on the data; encryption during rest and encryption during motion.

Encryption on data in rest means when the data is stored on a device. An example of this is using a BitLocker on your laptop's hard drive, or using the **Transparent Data Encryption (TDE)** in databases such as Oracle and SQL.

When the data is being transported (over the network), it is called data in motion, and two major protocols are used to encrypt the connection—IPSEC and SSL. An example of this is visiting `https://` websites, which encrypt the data using SSL.

Network perimeter security

Implementation of perimeter security is done using several products (majorly on the network space), including (but not limited to) firewalls, **Intrusion Detection and Prevention Systems (IDS/IPS)**, and proxies (web/reverse). Some of the perimeter security examples include **Web Application Firewall (WAF)** and many others.

Perimeter security also includes systems, such as antivirus, which are implemented with mail relay servers (to scan the emails being sent in and out), or with proxies to scan the websites that are being accessed.

Firewalls

These systems are used to allow/disallow the traffic between trusted and untrusted networks and they sit at the perimeter of a network. These networks also help in terminating an IPSEC connection between two sites, or even for remote access (remote access VPN).

The firewalls are normally stateful and support deep packet inspection for some protocols such as FTP, H323, and RPC. The recent firewalls now add features of other products such as IDS/IPS and antivirus, and are therefore called **Unified Threat Management (UTM)** devices. Some firewall examples are Cisco ASA, Juniper SRX, FortiGate, Check Point, and so on.

IDS/IPS

As the name suggests, these systems detect or protect against intrusion attempts made over the network. These devices can be at the network perimeter, called **Network IDS (NIDS)**, or on the hosts (servers) as **Host IDS (HIDS)**.

The systems use a combination of signature-based detection methods and analysis. Some examples of IDS and IPS systems are TippingPoint, Snort, Suricata, and so on.

Proxies

Web (HTTP/HTTPS) traffic has become the largest kind of traffic over the internet, and hence protecting these has become mandatory. A proxy is a device which acts as a client to the server and a server to the client.

The proxy has features such as the ability to block malicious websites by the usage of web-categorizing filters, and the ability to scan the content that is being received or being sent using an antivirus system.

Host controls

The host controls include systems that allow limited privilege escalation, such as sudo or power broker. It also includes host antivirus or internet security (which in turn includes host firewall, HIDS, and so on) such as Symantec or McAfee, anti-malware systems, and so on.

These systems also work on signature detection and heuristic algorithms, which allow us to detect a day-zero threat.

High availability and disaster recovery

These systems allow for the availability of the system in case of a disaster, which could be a cyber attack or a natural disaster. High availability allows for a more local fault (like a server going down), and disaster recovery systems allow for the failure of an entire data center.

Detection and analytics mechanism

One of the last steps in an attack that an attacker performs is setting up a backdoor, so that the attacker can be connected and also to cover their tracks. In order to prevent this from happening, logging everything centrally and allowing the logs to be searchable and made available for analytics is absolutely necessary. Systems such as Splunk, Graylog, ELK stack, and even Grafana (that we saw in the previous chapter) help us to do this.

Minimizing shared infrastructure

Minimizing the use of shared infrastructure between different companies or even different kinds of applications in the same organization helps reduce the attack surface, so that you may not be attacked using the type of vulnerabilities that were recently made public—Spectre and Meltdown.

Compliance standards and controls

Having taken a look at the basic concepts of security, it is now time that we take a look at compliance standards that are used in the industry and how some of the controls are implemented.

The compliance requirements can be for a particular industry, for example HIPAA for Healthcare, **PCI** for the **payment card industry**, and so on, or compliance requirements for a region, for example, the European Union has **General Data Protection Regulation (GDPR)**.

These standards have several aspects, including IT, process, and even documentation standards.

In the next section, we will take a look at the IT controls that need to be implemented for one of the compliance standards. I think HIPAA will be good as an example, due to its fairly comprehensive coverage and requirements.

HIPAA compliance standards

HIPAA is a standard for healthcare organizations in the US; however, most other healthcare institutions around the world are also influenced by the standards. While the standards are beyond the purview of the book, do read about them at the Health and Human Services website: https://www.hhs.gov/.

There are several controls that are needed for compliance, including (but not limited to):

- Administrative controls
- Physical controls
- Technical controls

We can find the full list of HIPAA controls at `https://www.hhs.gov/ hipaa/for-professionals/index.html`.

Administrative controls

As the name implies, these controls deal majorly with policies and processes. The major controls include:

- Security management policies that deal with risk analysis, risk management, and a policy to review the IT systems themselves
- Workforce security policies dealing with supervision, hiring, clearance, and termination processes of the workforce
- Information access management policies dealing with the authorization of accessing, establishing, and modifying it
- Security awareness training and evaluation policies
- Security incident policies about reporting and responding to the security incident

These policies are under the control of the chief security officer's team.

Physical controls

These controls deal with the physical access to the IT systems. The policies include the following:

- Data center facility access controls
- Workstation use and security policy
- Securing the workstation
- Controls pertaining to the disposal of IT systems

These include everything from access control to the premise using key cards and/or biometric authentication, to how old hard disks are to be disposed of.

Technical controls

These are the controls that are implemented by several products that we saw earlier. Let's take a look at the controls and the products required to implement them:

Controls	Example products	Remarks
Access control	Active Directory, LDAP, and so on	Each user will need a unique identifier to access the IT systems.
Automatic logoff	Active Directory Group Policy	Automatically log off the workstations when idle for a predetermined time.
Encryption/Decryption	BitLocker for hosts, TDE for database, key management system for storing the keys	The ability to encrypt the data so unauthorized access is prevented.
Audit controls	Syslog, Splunk, and ELK Stack	Log access to the systems and the data that was accessed. We also need to make the system immutable by the administrators so that they cannot make any modifications to the logs.
Transmission security	SSL certificates, IPSEC tunnels on firewalls	Ensure that the data is transmitted in an encrypted format.
Integrity	Active Directory, SAML, and Ocata	Ensure that the person who is accessing the system has authorization to do so.

There are several other controls (including ISO and NIST) in HIPAA. You can use a checklist provided at `https://www.healthit.gov/sites/default/files/tools/hit_security_risk_assessment_tool_v1.0_revised-1_0.xlsm` to get a more comprehensive checklist.

Security controls consideration in hybrid cloud

Since hybrid cloud is a combination of a private and a public cloud, we will divide this section into the parts and implement the controls individually in both of the clouds. We are again going to be using HIPAA as an example, as in the previous section, to elucidate our point.

Common controls

As we have already looked at HIPAA controls in the previous section, if we notice carefully, the administrative controls are something that are common to both the clouds. The policies will have to be made for the systems. Hence, we are adding that here. If the organization already has HIPAA compliance policies for the in-house data centers, the process for the public cloud can be appended and that should take care of it.

The technical controls are also common, as they might have a different implementation on different clouds. For example, we may use AWS Directory Service instead of Active Directory on the private cloud, but the concept remains the same.

Implementing the controls on AWS – public cloud

Since the administrative controls have been taken care of in a common fashion, we will deal with physical controls.

Since the public cloud is technically AWS's data center, the **physical controls** fall under the responsibility of AWS itself. AWS has certification on HIPAA for a list of services, which can be used and will clear the HIPAA requirements.

At the time of writing this book, 43 services out of hundreds of AWS services are eligible for HIPAA compliance. Refer to the updated list at `https://aws.amazon.com/compliance/hipaa-eligible-services-reference/`.

We can use these services and architect the application, and they can still be HIPAA-compliant.

> **FAQs on HIPAA on AWS:**
>
> `https://aws.amazon.com/blogs/security/frequently-asked-questions-about-hipaa-compliance-in-the-aws-cloud/`
>
> `https://aws.amazon.com/blogs/security/frequently-asked-questions-about-hipaa-compliance-in-the-aws-cloud-part-two/`

Security – shared responsibility model

AWS and every other public cloud provider works on the principle that security is a responsibility shared by us and the public cloud provider:

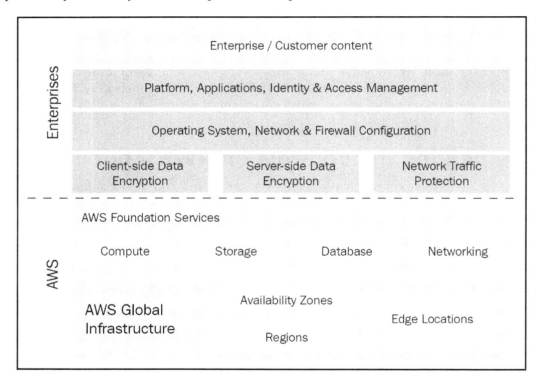

The responsibility of the security of the services in the Enterprises area belongs to us. The part under the AWS belongs to AWS. While all of the physical controls of HIPAA fall under AWS's purview, the technical controls are under our purview.

 Refer to the whitepaper for more information `https://d0.awsstatic.com/whitepapers/compliance/AWS_HIPAA_Compliance_Whitepaper.pdf`.

Implementing the controls in private cloud

Implementing the controls is not very different from implementing the controls on a traditional data center. Hence, in order to implement the controls, deploy the appropriate tools that were mentioned and configure the policies as required.

Security – best practices

Let's take a look at some of the best practices that can be considered while architecting the hybrid cloud environment.

Implementing a CMDB/asset list

It's a good idea to implement a **configuration management database (CMDB)** or an asset list with details as to what is running in each of the systems to ensure proper security controls can be put in place.

User accounts and authentication

We need to have best practices for user accounts and authentication policies. The best practices in this realm are as follows:

- **Multi-factor authentication**: We should enable multi-factor authentication, using products such as SecureID, or even some kind of a **Time-based One Time Password** (**TOTP**) such as Google Authenticator
- **Strong password policies**: We should set strong password policies for users in relation to password reuse, force password changes, length of passwords, and so on
- **Different privileged and normal accounts**: We should have different accounts for administrative users for performing administrative tasks; we should not provide administrative access to the normal user account that is created for them
- **Different directories/users for different environments**: We should ensure that different user accounts are used in different environments, so that even if one environment is compromised, the others remain unaffected

Provisioning and postprovisioning controls

In the hybrid cloud, we will be provisioning servers on both the private and the public cloud, hence some controls with regards to provisioning the systems are also to be taken into consideration:

- **Naming convention**:
  - A naming convention allows us to find out information about the server without logging into it; for example, consider the following naming convention and the details that it can provide without having to log in:
    - [LOC][O][E][APP][FUN][#]—LHRWPSHPWEB01:
      - LOC—location (LHR—London Heathrow)
      - O—operating system (W—Windows)
      - E—environment (P—production)
      - APP—application (SHP—SharePoint)
      - FUN—function (WEB—web server)
      - #—server number (01—first server)

- **IPAM**:
  - Have an **IP Address Management System (IPAM)** in order to help map the addresses that are being used
  - In the private cloud, this can be integrated into the provisioning process

- **Templates/Configuration management systems**:
  - Ensure that the templates that are being used are patched and ensure that they point to the appropriate servers (WSUS server in the case of Windows) for patching when they come to life
  - Ensure that the templates have appropriate antivirus, HIDS, and so on, systems installed on them, or ensure that the provisioning process connects to a configuration management system to install these

- **Disable unwanted services**:
  - We will need to ensure that any service that is not required is switched off, as doing this will reduce the attack surface

- **Root/Administrator accounts**:
  - Protect the root/administrator access, and don't allow direct access using the accounts remotely
- **Encryption**:
  - Encrypt the data in rest where applicable. This can be done by protecting the data drive with an encryption system.

Networks

The best practices for the network to be considered are as follows:

- **Using VLANs**:
  - Create virtual networks where possible. Virtual networks not only divide the broadcast domain, but also help segment the network from a security standpoint.
  - VLANs or Layer-2 networks can be easily created in a hybrid cloud mechanism.
- **Using perimeter security**:
  - Implement the perimeter security devices, as discussed in the previous sections, with stringent policies as applicable to your environment
- **Disabling unused ports**:
  - Disable any unused ports on the network as they may be used to plug in and gain access to the network, which may not be suitable
- **Performing network scans**:
  - Perform network vulnerability scanning at defined intervals and perform remediation where necessary

Other practices

Several other security best practices can be followed, some of them are enumerated here:

- Use a remote access VPN to provide access to remote workers
- Log everything in an immutable manner in a centralized location, and review the logs periodically
- Set up tape rotation for backup, and restrict access to the tapes

- Ensure the backups are encrypted and tested regularly
- Deploy the mail filtering application to protect from phishing, malware, and so on
- Use a central NTP server to synchronize the time everywhere
- Provide access with the Least Privilege mode, which simply means implicitly deny until the access is explicitly given

Summary

The preceding security principles and controls are merely guidelines that will help you get started on your security journey. The subject is vast, and hence you should follow the recommendations for further reading that have been provided.

Note that the snippets pertaining to security, which must be followed in every product we have used in the book, is mentioned in an information box or as a tip.

This brings us to the conclusion of our journey of architecting a hybrid cloud and some concepts in operating it. I sincerely hope that you enjoy reading it as much as I have writing it, and that it proves to be helpful to you.

Other Books You May Enjoy

If you enjoyed this book, you may be interested in these other books by Packt:

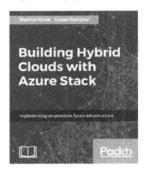

Building Hybrid Clouds with Azure Stack
Markus Klein, Susan Roesner

ISBN: 978-1-78646-629-7

- Gain a clear understanding of Azure Stack design
- Set up storage, network and compute services in Azure Stack
- Implement and run a hybrid cloud infrastructure with PaaS, SaaS, and IaaS services
- Get an overview of the automation options in Azure Stack
- Integrate Azure public services such as multi-factor authentication and Azure AD with Azure Stack
- Learn about the services available in the future

Azure for Architects
Ritesh Modi

ISBN: 978-1-78839-739-1

- Familiarize yourself with the components of the Azure Cloud platform
- Understand the cloud design patterns
- Use enterprise security guidelines for your Azure deployment
- Design and implement Serverless solutions
- See Cloud architecture and the deployment pipeline
- Understand cost management for Azure solutions

Leave a review - let other readers know what you think

Please share your thoughts on this book with others by leaving a review on the site that you bought it from. If you purchased the book from Amazon, please leave us an honest review on this book's Amazon page. This is vital so that other potential readers can see and use your unbiased opinion to make purchasing decisions, we can understand what our customers think about our products, and our authors can see your feedback on the title that they have worked with Packt to create. It will only take a few minutes of your time, but is valuable to other potential customers, our authors, and Packt. Thank you!

Index

solutions, using 201
use cases 39
Hypervisor 133

I

IaaC
  using, with Terraform 217
Identity and Access Management (IAM)
  about 73, 253
  Identity Federation 74
  Multi-Factor Authentication (MFA) 76
Identity provider (IdP) 75
independent software vendors (ISVs) 15
Infrastructure as a Code (IaaC) 211
infrastructure up clouds
  about 12
  and service down, difference 14
Internet Gateway (IGW) 98
Internet Key Exchange (IKE) 63
Internet Protocol Security (IPSec) 63
Intrusion Detection and Prevention Systems
  (IDS/IPS) 254
IP Address Management System (IPAM) 262
isolated/distributed application use case
  about 128
  ICMP, general architecture 129
  ManageIQ 130
  Northbound APIs 128
  Southbound APIs 128

J

Juju client
  installing 172
Juju controller
  accessing, with GUI 177
Juju
  reference 180
  used, for deploying Kubernetes 178

K

kernel 134
kernel namespace 134
KubeFed
  reference 184

Kubernetes clusters
  connecting to 183
Kubernetes deployment
  Juju 170
Kubernetes federation, challenges
  consolidations, monitoring 189
  public cloud data-transfer costs 189
  reliability and latency considerations 189
Kubernetes federation
  challenges 189
  creating 193
  DNS provider, creating 193
  federation controller, setting up 190
  implementing 189
  initializing 193
  Kubernetes configuration, combining 191
  reference 189
Kubernetes
  about 164
  cloud bursting 188
  concepts 166
  consideration, reasons 185
  controllers 167
  deploying, with Juju 178
  deployment 170
  Federation service 184
  high availability 188
  master node 165
  namespaces 168
  pod 166
  policies, enforcing 186
  reference 170
  second instance, deploying 181
  service 167
  upgrades 188
  vendor lock-in, avoiding 186
  volumes 167
  worker node 165

L

load balancers 46
load-kubeconfig tool 191
log shipping 80

www.ingramcontent.com/pod-product-compliance
Lightning Source LLC
Chambersburg PA
CBHW080630060326
40690CB00021B/4875